Praise for *Can Do Writing*

"*Can Do Writing* is excellent for scientists who write to managers and clients. The specific techniques especially help writers like me who write technical English as a second language."

—*Cindy Xinguang Li*
PhD in Pharmacology and Toxicology

"I have transformed my writing after using the Grahams' methods. Now, my managers applaud my writing. I recommend strongly this logical, ten-step approach to anyone who writes for business, government, or non-profit organizations."

—*Padmaja Mummaneni*
PhD in Biology and Life Sciences, Delhi University

"*Can Do Writing's* friendly design and practical examples ease the reader into an intimate look at written communication. We implement the *Can Do Writing* system into our curriculum worldwide."

—*Skip Pettit*
president, International Training Consortium, Inc.

"*Can Do Writing* is the finest book on writing I have read—the essence of writing well. Time-pressed people who read this book on a cross-country flight will be far better writers when they land."

—*Larry Tracy*
president, Tracy Presentation Skills

CAN DO
WRITING™

CAN DO
WRITING™

The Proven Ten-Step
System for Fast and
Effective Business
Writing

Daniel Graham, MBA and
Judith Graham, PhD

WILEY

John Wiley & Sons, Inc.

Published by John Wiley & Sons, Inc., Hoboken, New Jersey.
Published simultaneously in Canada.

For general information on our other products and services or for technical support, please
contact our Customer Care Department within the United States at (800) 762-2974,
outside the United States at (317) 572-3993, or fax (317) 572-4002.

Wiley publishes in a variety of print and electronic formats and by print-on-demand. Some
material included with standard print versions of this book may not be included in e-books
or in print-on-demand. If this book refers to media such as a CD or DVD that is not included
in the version you purchased, you may download this material at http://booksupport.wiley.com.
For more information about Wiley products, visit www.wiley.com.

Library of Congress Cataloging-in-Publication Data:

Graham, Daniel, 1952–
    Can do writing : the proven ten-step system for fast and effective business writing / by
Daniel Graham and Judith Graham.
       p. cm.
    Includes index.
    ISBN 978-0-470-44979-0 (pbk.)
    1. Business writing. I. Graham, Judith, 1952–   II. Title.
    HF5718.3.G73   2009
    651.7'4—dc22
                                            2008045571

10 9 8 7 6 5 4 3 2 1

*We dedicate this book to our clients
with sincere thanks to them all.*

Engineering, Manufacturing, Business
AKZO NOBEL — Intervet, Inc.
Applied Ordnance Technology, Inc.
BAE Systems, Inc.
Barrett Penan & Company
Booz Allen Hamilton
Bureau of National Affairs
Celfocus, Portugal
CGI-American Management Systems
Christopher Consulting, Inc.
Computer Sciences Corporation
Constellation Energy
Covance Laboratories
Database Management, Inc.
DCI Group, Inc.
Dialogic Corporation
Ernst & Young
Evans, Inc.
Forrester Construction
Global eXchange Services
Goodman & Company
Hechts
Heckler and Koch U.S.A.
JAYCOR

Lockheed-Martin
Mitchell Systems, Inc.
MITRE Corporation
Mitretek Systems
Northrop Grumman
Pharmaceutical Research and Manufacturers of America (PhRMA)
Price Waterhouse LLP
QinetiQ
Reznick Group
RGS, Inc.
Slone Partners
SOVRAN Bank
Sterling Software
T.A. Carlson
Teledyne Brown Engineering
TESS, Inc.
The Discovery Channel
Touchstone, Inc. – SRA, Inc.
TRW, Inc.
Vector Research, Inc.

Government
Department of Health and Human Services
    Health and Human Services University
    Health Resource and Services Administration
    Administration for Children and Families
    Centers for Medicare and Medicaid Services
    Asst. Secretary for Resources and Technology
Environmental Protection Agency
Federal Aviation Agency
Joint National Integration Center (JNIC)
NASA Goddard Space Flight Center

National Geospatial-Intelligence Agency (NGA)
National Institutes of Health
    Center for Scientific Review
    National Cancer Institute
    National Library of Medicine
Naval Surface Warfare Center
Prince William Co. Criminal Justice Academy
U.S. Food and Drug Administration
    Office of the Commissioner
    Office of Management
    Center for Drug Evaluation and Research
    Center for Devices and Radiological Health
    Center for Biologics Evaluation and Research
    Center for Veterinary Medicine
U.S. Government Printing Office
U.S. Patent and Trademark Office
U.S. Public Building Services-GSA
Veterans Administration
Virginia Department of Transportation

Nonprofit Organizations
American Public Transportation Association
Baltimore-Washington Information Systems Educators
Center for International Private Enterprise
Center for Smart Business Policy
Georgetown University Foreign Service Program
INROADS, Inc.
Leadership Institute
National Housing Partnership
The National Rifle Association

We also thank our agent Lila Karpf—wisdom is priceless.

Contents

Preface

Do you find yourself on the following list? If so, *Can Do Writing* is right for you:

- Business professional who wants to satisfy customers while working more efficiently and reducing risks.
- Subject matter expert who wants to write clear advice to your manager or client who might not be an expert in your subject.
- Recent college graduate who wants to learn how to write to an audience at work, instead of a professor in a classroom.
- Scientist or engineer who proposes funding for your next project.
- Engineer who wants to instruct others in how to design, build, use, or maintain your system.
- Scientist who wants to share your exciting discovery in the laboratory with the larger scientific community.
- Public relations or sales representative who needs to persuade.
- Project manager who manages a team of writers and editors.
- Accountant who wants to write your audit reports clearly and quickly.
- Administrative assistant who wants to make sure that your letter gets every attendee to the conference on time and with ease.
- Professional who speaks and writes English as a second language.
- Government professional who writes policies, plans, budgets, or reports.

Daniel Graham holds a Master's Degree in Business Administration from the University of Alabama. For 15 years, he worked on large documentation projects in the U.S. Army and in high tech consulting firms. His work is published in trade and peer review journals ranging from law, finance, and accounting to risk management and engineering. He was the founder and managing editor of the *Journal of Practical Applications in Space*. He is an award-winning author of five science-fiction novels.

Judith Graham earned her PhD in English Literature at the University of Maryland. For ten years, she taught writing at the University of Alabama, the University of Texas, the University of Maryland, and George Mason University. She edits trade publications, technical digests, and other peer review journals. Her work is published in IEEE Transactions and in literary and training publications.

The Grahams started Graham Associates in 1985 to provide quality consulting and training for engineers, scientists, and business professionals. To date, they have taught more than 70,000 professionals in their writing seminars. Many of their clients have formally adopted the Grahams' writing system into their best practices.

CAN DO
WRITING™

Introduction

Can Do Writing

Can Do Writing helps you get the job done when you write. No matter what your occupation, product, or service, with the *Can Do Writing* system you write successful documents in less time. The system's ten steps work through analysis, composing the draft, and editing. For each step, you use proven techniques—46 in all. These techniques are easy to learn and apply. They work for every kind of nonfiction document: from simple reports to complex proposals, informal e-mails to formal journal articles.

Can Do Writing is about getting results. You *can do* your job, writing a purposeful document. Your document *can do* its job by providing your audience the necessary information: organized, clear, concise, and easy to read. Then your audience *can do* its job by using the information in your document. If you discover the cure for cancer, but you can't write your findings so others can use your information, all your time in the lab may be wasted, your discovery lost. Professionals who can write useful documents are the most valuable.

Can Do Writing helps you write faster. You can quickly and systematically analyze your writing situation, compose your draft with confidence, and edit. You avoid time-consuming rewrites. When you use the system, you can manage your time and meet deadlines.

Never be intimidated by writing again: By using the *Can Do Writing* system, you have control. You can break the daunting work of writing into manageable tasks. You understand the logic of documents so you don't simply mimic other, often poorly written, documents. You know how to find and fix problems early.

One of the best features of writing systematically is that as writers we can see our own improvement. Every document is an

3

opportunity to improve. Although we do not let the *perfect* be the *enemy* of the good, we keep improving. Within a week of using the *Can Do Writing* system, you will see marked improvement in your writing, and you get the satisfaction of knowing that you continue to improve your writing throughout your career.

You can start using these techniques today. You do not need a strong background in English grammar to follow the ten steps and use the techniques. You have a purpose for writing and information other people need. Now, learn the *Can Do Writing* system and apply the steps with confidence as you write your way to success.

Overview of *Can Do Writing* System

Many writers feel overwhelmed by writing. They say, I have writer's block. I don't know where to start. I get contradictory directions on what to write. My boss doesn't understand what I mean. I get swamped by the little details of grammar and punctuation. And it takes too much time to write—time I need to spend on other parts of my job.

These writers are overwhelmed because they don't have a system. Writing requires making hundreds of practical decisions, and these overwhelmed writers are trying to make all those decisions at the same time. They might as well try to juggle a hundred balls. *Can Do Writing* helps writers make the right decisions in the right order, with precision and speed.

First, we need to separate those hundreds of decisions into three skillsets: analysis, composing the draft, and editing.

To understand how these skillsets affect writing, let's compare writing a document to building a house. First, the builder starts with analysis, designing the house to satisfy the homeowners' needs and meet building standards. The builder uses a blueprint to record the analysis. Second, the builder constructs the house, working quickly to frame the structure, raise the roof, and seal the structure. Third, the builder adds the finishing touches such as crown molding, paint, and carpets.

Imagine if a builder, without a blueprint, builds a house from left to right, room by room, trying to make each room perfect before moving to the next. Analyze one room; construct one room; finish one room. This approach is slow and expensive. Moreover, the house lacks structural integrity and will probably fall down.

Unfortunately, most writers make the mistake of mixing skillsets. They try to analyze and edit while composing the draft. Without a sentence outline, they attempt to write a document from top to bottom, paragraph by paragraph, trying to make each paragraph perfect before moving to the next. They are quickly overwhelmed, and the result is much wasted time, frustration, and often a poor document.

To work efficiently, the writer—like the builder—needs to work systematically. The writer analyzes the audience's needs. The analysis takes the form of a sentence outline instead of a blueprint. Next, the efficient writer composes the rough draft, much like the builder's rough carpentry work. Finally, the efficient writer systematically edits the document—putting on the finishing touches.

The *Can Do Writing* system has ten steps, organized into three skillsets:

Analysis—Steps 1 through 4

In four easy steps, you can successfully analyze *any* writing situation. These steps lead you through the right questions in the right order, starting with "What result do you want from the document?" You select the correct type of document for each audience. You get to the point immediately while managing your tone. You select the right facts, then organize your points in a sentence outline. You can settle controversies early before you invest time composing and editing a draft.

Composing—Step 5

In this step, you learn the most efficient order for composing the draft: body, conclusion, and introduction. Also, you learn the formats for introductions, summaries, and abstracts.

The key to composing the draft is doing the analysis first. As you fill in your outline with supporting facts, work quickly; do not stop to edit. Premature editing is inefficient—the *biggest* waste of time when writing a document—yet most writers make this mistake. After you learn to edit systematically, you can easily resist editing as you compose the draft.

Editing—Steps 6 through 10

Editing is mechanical. These steps ensure that your document has purpose, is logical, well organized, clear, concise, and easy to read. You apply techniques systematically because the steps build on each other. For example, in Step 6, you review the document to ensure that the facts are correct and the logic is good. Now that you are sure you have a factually correct, logical draft, you can proceed to Step 7 to add coherence devices to make the logic more obvious to the reader.

In Steps 8 through 10, you perform three edits to ensure that your sentences are clear, concise, and easy to read. Again, these steps build on each other. As you learn these steps, you see that editing for clarity automatically makes the document more concise. Editing for economy automatically makes the document easier to read. Finally, editing for readability ensures that your document text is at the grade level your reader expects.

Checking for Correctness

After you apply *Can Do Writing's* systematic editing techniques, you correct word choice, grammar, punctuation, and mechanics. You consult dictionaries, reference manuals, and style guides that we do not replicate in this book. Finally, you *proofread* to catch flaws such as typographical errors. Save valuable time by checking for correctness and proofreading *after* your document is coherent, clear, concise, and easy to read.

Skillset: Analysis

If you don't know where you're going, you might not get there.
—Yogi Berra

With the *Can Do Writing* system, you analyze your writing situation *before* you commit to the hard work of composing the draft and editing.

Analysis has four steps. First, you analyze purpose and audience so you know the desired results and the information needed to get those results. Second, you write a five-part purpose statement to focus your efforts and then focus the reader. Third, you select the facts your audience needs. Fourth, you organize your points in a sentence outline, turning facts into useful information.

These steps build on each other. In this skillset, we teach Steps 1 and 2, then practice with a business case study. Then we teach Steps 3 and 4, pausing again to practice all four steps with another case study.

You can skip analysis for only two reasons. If you are a genius like Wolfgang Amadeus Mozart, you do not need systematic analysis, nor do you need to read this book. Also, you don't need systematic analysis if your document is a fill-in-the-blank template designed to capture data, not ideas—like a bank loan application. The bank did all the analysis for you by preparing the template; you just fill in the facts.

Otherwise, do not skip analysis. In our experience working with professionals, more than 90 percent of all ineffective documents fail because the author either skipped or took shortcuts in analysis.

Your analysis produces a sentence outline—the blueprint for your document. The first sentence in your outline is your document's purpose statement. The purpose statement determines whether the rest of the information in the document is relevant—a key to writing logical and persuasive documents. The rest of your outline is a series of short sentences—the points you need to make to accomplish what you propose in the purpose statement.

Your word processor is not a good tool for analysis. The word processor lures you into composing the draft before you finish the outline—wasting time and effort. Pen and paper are better tools for analysis.

Take Yogi's advice. Make sure you know where you—*the writer*—are going and that you take your readers where they need to go.

Analyze Purpose and Audience

To start planning your document, answer six questions in order as you analyze purpose and audience. Treat each question as a necessary technique. One question is about you, the writer: What result do you want? Five questions are about your audience. If you can't answer the following six analytical questions, you can't write a successful document:

1.1 What result do you want from the document?
1.2 Who is the audience?
1.3 What does the audience do with the information?
1.4 What information does the audience need?
1.5 Does the audience know little or much about the information?
1.6 Does the audience need proof?

For recent college graduates entering the workplace, analysis is key to making the transition between academic essays and results-oriented documents. In school, you pay other people to read your documents. Now that you are out of school, you want other people to pay you to write documents. They are not going to read your documents or pay you unless your documents have value for them. These six techniques ensure that your documents provide value to your reader.

Analysis of your purpose and the audience helps you make important decisions about the document. You decide the type of document to write. You manage the tone of your document—neutral to authoritative. You identify the information the audience needs to achieve its purpose, and consequently you know what is relevant. What the audience does with the information provides clues on how best to organize the document. If the audience knows little about the information, you need to write a longer document—often twice as long. If the audience needs proof, you need to write a longer document including more supporting facts.

For some complex documents, you may have more than one audience. If you have more than one audience, you need to analyze each separately. We provide examples of multiple audiences in this step. Each has a different purpose; each needs different information. One audience knows a little while the other knows much. One audience needs proof while the other does not. Later, you write to each separately, either in separate documents or in separate sections within a document. If you have more than one audience, add a seventh technique:

1.7 Plan how to write to multiple audiences.

1.1 What Result Do You Want from the Document?

When we ask writers what *result* they want from their document, we usually get answers like, "I want to inform . . . explain . . . describe. . . ." Okay, but *why* do you want to *inform, explain,* or *describe*? What *result* do you want?

Result? Some writers think self-interest is wrong—as if wanting a result is impolite. If the result is good, what is wrong with wanting it? The job seeker wants the satisfying job. The contracting officer wants the best value at the least risk. The sales staff wants to sell their goods and services. Staff experts want managers to accept their recommendations. Managers want their plans and decisions implemented.

Most successful business relationships occur when two parties participate in an activity that helps both get the result each wants. Likewise, documents succeed when the document helps the writer and reader both get the result each wants.

Therefore, know what result you want, and don't be altruistic. *My company wants to inform the client of a new upgrade* is altruistic. Instead, identify what result you want from the document: *We want the client to buy the new hardware upgrade from us.*

Subject matter experts often focus on subject matter instead of what result they want: *My purpose is to explain the functions of the new billing system.* Why are you explaining the functions? Instead, focus on the result you achieve with your explanation: *I want the client to approve the billing system functions, so my technical staff can develop a detailed design.*

Never vent feelings: *I'm expressing my outrage at the unauthorized charge on my credit card account.* So what if you're outraged? Instead, focus on the result you want: *I want the credit card company to remove the unauthorized charge from my account.*

Be sure to limit the result you expect from any specific document. For example, you want a job that you see advertised. So you submit your resume with a cover letter. Don't write, *Please review my resume and send me a job offer.* The purpose of the cover letter is simply to inform the company that you are applying and to encourage them to read your resume. The purpose of your resume is to get an interview. The purpose of the interview is to get a job offer.

The result you want from the document affects the kind of document you choose, such as e-mail, letter, report, or proposal. *The result you want* also affects your tone, such as formal, informal, warm, or firm.

If you write for someone else's signature—your boss' perhaps—ensure that you know what result the boss wants from the document. Don't guess.

1.2 Who Is the Audience?

Having decided what you want from the document, turn your attention to the audience. First, answer this question: *Who is the audience?* The audience is whoever *uses* the document's information to do something. Your audience can be a single reader or a group of readers with similar needs. If you misidentify the audience, your document is a failure from the start.

If you don't know who uses the information, don't guess: Ask.

Organization charts do not determine your audience. Organization charts may determine how you route your communication, but not necessarily who uses it. For example, you work in the U.S. Patent and Trademark Office. You get a letter from Senator Smith asking you to explain how his constituent, Mr. Jones, can get an extension on a patent. A copy of Mr. Jones' letter is attached. Protocol dictates that you reply to the senator, but you need to direct the information to Mr. Jones, who uses the information. For example, *Dear Senator Smith: This letter explains how your constituent Mr. Jones can apply for an extension for his patent. . . .*

Therefore, do not assume that your boss is the audience. Often, the boss does not use the information. Rather, the boss provides quality control for your document.

Be specific when identifying your audience. For example, you are the office manager of Temps & Co., a temporary employment agency. You write a policy that begins, *This policy describes our company benefits for employees. . . .* In this case, the audience *employees* is too general. Instead, write, *This policy describes our company benefits for full-time employees.* By being specific, you avoid making trouble for yourself and your temporary employees, who cannot use the information in the document.

A document may have more than one audience. For example, technical manuals often have multiple audiences: The user reads the manual to use the tool, while the technician uses the manual to maintain the tool. When writing a large proposal, you often have multiple audiences: users, contract officers, budget specialists, and legal staff. Staff studies often have two audiences. the managers who decide and the experts who advise managers what to decide.

Remember, if you have multiple audiences, you must analyze each separately. Later in technique 1.7, you plan how to accommodate each audience with separate documents or sections.

1.3 What Does the Audience Do with the Information?

To analyze each audience, begin by answering the question: *What does the audience do with the information?* What the audience does with the information is the most important piece of the analysis. Be specific with your answer. Think past the obvious, "The audience reads and evaluates. . . ." Exactly *what do they do* with the information that they read and evaluate?

If you don't know what the audience does with the information in your document, don't guess: find out. Everything in your document is relevant only to the extent that it helps the audience do whatever they need to do. If you don't know what they do with the information, you cannot possibly know what information they need.

In general, readers do three things with information:

1. Advise others
2. Decide, which includes plan, budget, and manage
3. Follow instructions to perform tasks

Consider, for example, information about wireless computer networks. A company's technology expert uses technical information to advise management about choosing a wireless network. A manager uses information about the costs and benefits to decide whether to convert to a wireless network. Employees use *how to* information to share files on the wireless network.

How people use information is independent of job titles and education. Every person at every level gives advice, makes decisions, and follows instructions.

Don't waste time writing a document that lacks purpose. If the reader doesn't see the purpose, then your document is by default an FYI (for your information) document. How do readers react to FYI documents? When you sort through your e-mails, what do you do when you suspect an e-mail is just FYI? If you are like most busy people, you hit the delete key so fast that you approach the speed of light. Serious people ignore purposeless FYI documents.

Avoid vague descriptions of the audience's purpose:

This brochure helps students understand the enrollment process. (*vague*)
This brochure tells the student how to enroll for summer classes. (*specific*)

Remember, if you have multiple audiences, determine what each does with the document. For example, you work for a drug company, writing text about a new drug for your company web site. You have two audiences: the public and physicians. The public reads the text so they can consult their physicians. Physicians read so they can safely prescribe the drug.

1.4 What Information Does the Audience Need?

What the audience *does* with the information determines what information they *need*. Do not tell them everything you know, just what they need.

We must contrast writing in school and writing in the workplace. In school we learned *more is better.* We tried to impress the teacher with how much we knew about the subject. In fact, we earned better grades when we demonstrated the breadth of our knowledge. However, in the workplace, readers do not care how much we know unless that knowledge helps them do something. In school, we learned, *if you can't answer the question, answer a question you can.* That strategy is reasonable when taking a test. However, in the workplace, when we can't answer the question, the smart response is, *I don't know. I will find an answer.*

Much of the value you, as a subject-matter expert, provide the audience is your ability to select the necessary information from the vast store of unnecessary information. Usually the audience needs to know a small subset of what you know about the subject. They just want the information they need to accomplish some particular purpose. Everything else you know about the subject is irrelevant in the document.

Imagine that you are the inventor of a ceramic paint that lasts 30 years. You proved scientifically that your paint works. Now you need to raise capital to build a manufacturing plant. You prepare a briefing to present your promising technology to Venture Capital Inc., who can raise the capital you need. Venture Capital does not need to know how you make your paint. Moreover, they don't really care how you make your paint. They need to know the capital required, the potential return on investment, the schedule of payback, and the risks.

If you don't know whether the audience needs to know something, ask them.

If you have multiple audiences who do different things with the information, you can be certain they need different information.

1.5 Does the Audience Know Little or Much About the Information?

Citing *only* what information the audience needs, answer the question: *Does the audience know little or much about the information?*

For example, you write a staff study comparing *the cost to lease or buy* a Cessna Citation CJ2 2000 corporate jet, so your company treasurer can present the idea to the board of directors. The treasurer knows next to nothing about jets, but she doesn't need information about jets. Rather, she needs information about leasing and buying. Therefore, she knows much. On the other hand, if the company pilot reads the same document, he knows little: He knows much about jet aircraft but not finance.

If the audience knows much about the information, you can use technical language, even jargon. If the audience knows little, you help them in four ways:

1. Define words.
2. Give examples.
3. Provide analogies.
4. Draw pictures.

You might think your audience is halfway between knowing little and much—indeed, most people are between. Nevertheless, you need to pick *little* or *much* because you can't give *half*-definitions, *half*-examples, *half*-analogies, or *half*-pictures.

The audience who knows little *always* gets a longer document, often two to three times longer than the same document written to an audience who knows much. Use this valuable insight to help you estimate the time for any writing task.

If you don't know if the audience knows little or much, ask if they want you to define words, give examples, or provide analogies and pictures. If you can't ask and must guess, always guess that the audience knows much. You get in as much or more trouble for writing a document too long as writing a document too short. First, you spend two to three times the labor hours writing the long document—time you cannot get back. Second, managers resent reading long documents written beneath them, and they rightly assume that they are paying more for a long document when they want a less expensive short document. The wiser approach is to send the short document written for the audience who knows much. Let the manager ask you for the longer version.

Whether the audience knows little or much about the subject affects the type of document you choose, the length of the document, and your word choice.

1.6 Does the Audience Need Proof?

Based only on what the audience needs to know, answer the question: *Does the audience need proof?* If they need proof, you need to include more supporting facts.

Don't assume that you must prove everything. People hire experts for their expert advice, not for their detailed proofs.

The audience who needs proof always gets a longer document, because they need more supporting details. Use this valuable insight to help you budget your time for any writing task.

If you don't know whether the audience needs proof, ask. If you can't ask, always assume the audience believes you. You save time. Moreover, managers under time-pressure to make a decision resent experts who force them to read detailed proofs. Software users who want simple instructions groan when the manual explains the clever design and engineering subtleties in the software.

Sometimes the audience who wants proof won't understand the proof. A common scenario involves the manager who needs to know the business impact (the effect) of a decision. Also, the manager wants proof. Unfortunately, the proof is usually in the science or technology (the cause).

For example, a sales manager wants to decide whether investing in an interactive web site can improve customer service. He needs information about costs, benefits to his customers and sales staff, and reliability. He is skeptical about *machines* interacting with his customers, so he wants proof. The proof is in a detailed discussion of computer science: hardware, software, and communications. The sales manager knows almost nothing about computer science; however, the company has a computer expert on staff. Writing the proof to the sales manager is a waste of time.

Therefore, write about web-based customer support in two parts—one part to each audience. Write about the business impact (the effect) to the sales manager who makes the decision. Write about the technical proof (the cause) to the computer expert who advises the sales manager.

Whether the audience needs proof affects the type of document you choose, amount of supporting detail, and tone.

1.7 Plan How to Write to Multiple Audiences.

If you discover that your document has more than one audience, apply this seventh technique: Plan how to write to your multiple audiences. You must write to each separately. You cannot write to different audiences in the same body of a document.

Audiences have different—*usually incompatible*—needs. The manager and the staff expert read for different reasons. They need different information. They know much about their own jobs and perhaps little about the other's job. They may have different requirements for proof. Conversely, if readers share the same reason for reading, need the same information, have the same level of knowledge and requirements for proof—they are actually just one audience.

Use any combination of these three ways to separate information for different audiences:

1. Write separate documents.
2. Break your document into sections, each serving a different audience.
3. Use transmittal letters, summaries, abstracts, appendices, attachments, exhibits, notes, and glossaries for different audiences.

How you separate the information for the audiences is judgment. For example, you use separate documents when you prefer that the audiences not see each other's information. You use sections when the different audiences need access to each other's information. If you use sections for each audience, each section has its own introduction, body, and conclusion. Use transmittal letters, summaries, and abstracts to help readers who might not want to read the entire document. Use the appendices, attachments, exhibits, notes, glossaries, and indexes after the main document to help readers who need supplementary information. Notes can also appear at the bottom of the pages or in shadow boxes in the main document.

For example, if your primary audience is a technical expert, write the document using jargon and theory, but add an executive summary for the manager and a glossary for the less technical audience. However, if your primary audience is the manager who has a general knowledge of the subject, put the technical details, jargon, and theory in an appendix for the staff experts.

Sometimes one audience knows little and another knows much about the information in the document. A typical example is a user manual where some users already know much about the system and others know little. You accommodate each by writing the thorough step-by-step manual with pictures for the audience who knows little; then add a quick reference guide as an appendix for the audience who knows much.

2 Write Your Document's Five-Part Purpose Statement

After analyzing purpose and audience, write a five-part purpose statement that defines the *purpose* of your document. You use the purpose statement to focus yourself as you write. Later, you make the purpose statement the first sentence in the introduction to focus the reader. If the reader doesn't quickly understand the *purpose* for the document, the information seems irrelevant, and therefore illogical. Indeed, the purpose statement is the most important sentence in the document.

Here are the five parts of the purpose statement in a typical order, plus an example:

1. Type of document—report.
2. What the document does—describes.
3. What information the audience needs—three energy-saving tips.
4. The audience—homeowners.
5. What the audience does with the information—reduce utility bills.

This report (*type of document*) describes (*what the document does*) three energy-saving tips (*information the audience needs*) homeowners (*the audience*) can use to reduce utility bills (*what the audience does*).

Step 2 builds on the analysis of Step 1. In Step 1, you analyzed your audience and developed three of the five parts of the purpose statement: *who is the audience, what the audience does with the information,* and *what information the audience needs.* In Step 2, you make two decisions about the document: *type of document* and *what the document does.*

These two decisions provide the remaining two parts you need before you assemble and use your five-part purpose statement.

Step 2 has four techniques:

2.1 Decide the type of document or oral communication to use.
2.2 Pick a verb that describes what the document does.
2.3 Assemble the five parts into a purpose statement.
2.4 Use the purpose statement to settle controversies.

Don't obsess over word choice yet. You can edit later. Linguists calculate that for any English text of 26 words, there are more than *six billon* ways to write the same thing. If you are obsessing about which is the best of the six billion ways, you need a hobby.

Master the five-part purpose statement. Your documents get to the point, manage tone, and convince the reader.

2.1 Decide the Type of Document or Oral Communication to Use.

Decide the type of document you need to write by recalling your analysis of audience. Is your audience one person or many? Is the information they need complex? Do they know little? Do they need proof? You might decide to communicate your message orally: a briefing, telephone call, or private conversation.

Written communication has three advantages:

1. Accuracy—you can provide many details with precision.
2. Economy—you can reach many readers with the same message.
3. Record—you can provide an audit trail or record for future readers.

Oral communication has two advantages:

1. Instant feedback—your audience can participate.
2. Privacy—you can limit exposure.

Your relationship with the audience determines if you need to use formal correspondence or a less formal e-mail or phone call. For example, letters sent outside the organization are more formal than internal memos. A sales brochure to the public is less formal than a proposal letter to the U.S. Government.

Don't hide behind documents. For example, your employee Bob comes to work late five days in a row. Too many managers send a generic memo to staff, reminding *everyone* to come to work on time. The result is an insult to the prompt employees. Also, the generic memo takes a potentially private matter and makes it public. As an effective manager, you do the analysis. You want Bob to come to work on time. The audience is Bob—just Bob. He uses the information to keep his job. He knows much about the subject (he can tell time), and he had better believe you. Consequently, you decide to discuss the matter with Bob in a private conversation, and if necessary, record the discussion with a memo to his file.

Don't document everything. You may unwittingly document a conflict best forgotten. Never argue in an e-mail. At the first whiff of an argument, pick up the phone and call. Never write anything you don't want read back to you in court.

Be as specific as possible as you name the document. *Memo, letter, message, note, staff study, marketing plan, business plan, budget, proposal, trip report, audit, resume, manual, policy, procedure, guidance*—just knowing the kind of document prepares the reader for the document's length, information, organization, and formality.

2.2 Pick a Verb That Describes What the Document Does.

For the final part of your purpose statement, you pick the verb that describes what the document *does*, so the audience *can do* something.

Do not pick a verb that describes what *you* as writer do. For example, avoid having your document *recommend, persuade, demand, promise,* or *study.* A promise coming from a piece of paper is not as persuasive as a promise made by a person or an organization with a reputation to defend. Therefore, your purpose statement says, *This letter describes our customer-satisfaction guarantee,* and later in the body you make the point, *We promise to beat any competitor's published price or refund you 110 percent of the difference.*

The verb you choose sets expectations. *This letter describes* is appropriate for an audience who knows a lot and simply needs descriptions. *This letter explains* suggests that the audience knows little and needs explanations. *This letter highlights* or *summarizes* sets the expectation—not many detailed proofs here. *This letter details* prepares the reader to expect many details.

The verb you choose needs to work with *the information the audience needs.* For example, your employees need to know how to calculate the number of exemptions when submitting a W-2 form to the Internal Revenue Service. The verb *suggests* doesn't work: *This memo suggests how you calculate the number of exemptions. . . .* The verb *suggests* implies alternatives. A better verb is *describes.*

The verb you pick sets the *tone* for your document. Think of tone as the attitude one hears in your voice. Readers sense a tone in your words. *This letter informs* or *presents* is neutral. *This letter notifies* sounds official and infers that the reader now has the responsibility to act. *This letter alerts* or *warns* has a forceful tone. Sometimes you need to be forceful for the reader's sake: *This letter warns you that if you do not pay your power bill within 30 days, we plan to cut your power.*

The purpose statement ensures that you begin with a professional and never egotistical tone. The document is all about *you the reader*, not all about *me the writer*. A document that starts, *I am writing to inform about our new product*, has an egotistical tone, focusing on the writer. Instead, use a purpose statement: *This letter describes how you can save time and money using our new product.*

The first impression is the most important. After you set the tone with the purpose statement, you can stop worrying about the tone of your document.

2.3 Assemble the Five Parts into a Purpose Statement.

Now you assemble the five parts into a purpose statement:

1. Type of document.
2. What the document does.
3. What information the audience needs.
4. The audience.
5. What the audience does with the information.

Type of document. Audiences, especially within organizations, expect similar formats for standard documents. Each type of document sets different expectations, whether staff study, report, review, white paper, proposal, functional description, test plan, user manual, guidance, policy, procedure, letter, memo, or e-mail.

What the document does. The verb you select sets the tone and helps set expectations. The verb tells what the document does—not what the writer does.

Audience. The reader quickly learns if he or she is the intended audience. By stating the audience, you help your readers and yourself. If a document is silent about audience, the reader assumes that he or she is the intended audience: *It's in my inbox after all.* Unintended readers often get frustrated because the information is irrelevant or not appropriate to their level of knowledge. They criticize—and rightly so—the writer. Readers who learn from the purpose statement that they are not the intended audience read at their own risk, and do not blame the writers.

Information the audience needs. The reader quickly learns the broad topics of the information in the document in the order presented. For example, if the information topics are *transportation and storage costs*, the reader expects to learn about transportation costs first, storage costs second—not about requirements or technology—just costs.

What the audience does with the information. Recall that if you omit *what the audience does with the information*, you by default write a *for-your-information-only* document that most readers ignore. For emphasis, you can presume the outcome you want. For example, *This letter details the costs of outsourcing our payroll, so management can justify keeping payroll in house.* The purpose statement presumes that management makes the decision we want: *keeping payroll in house.*

Assemble the five parts into a sentence or two. Sometimes *what the audience does with the information* is complicated, and sometimes *the information the audience needs* is complicated. Be flexible. Arrange the five parts in any order. Don't worry about editing the purpose statement yet: You waste time if you do. Whereas the five parts are important, the exact wording is not. A purpose statement can be two sentences:

This change proposal (*type of document*) presents (*what the document does*) the cost and schedule impact of adding customer online banking to the web site (*information the audience needs*). Universe Bank (*audience*) needs to decide whether to expand the scope of our contract or keep the original contract schedule (*what audience does with the information*).

In *how to* documents, the *how to* is the information the reader needs, and the action that follows the *how to* is what the reader does:

> This user guide (*type of document*) informs (*what the document does*) new employees (*audience*) how to (*information the audience needs*) enroll in the company's health insurance plan (*what audience does with the information*).

Sometimes parts of a purpose statement are self-evident. In a letter, the audience might be evident from the salutation. In advertisements or newsletter articles, the document type is self-evident. Include these parts as you first describe your purpose statement. You can discard them in the final draft if they are self-evident, as in this example:

> Are you over 65, in good health, (*audience*) and looking for a way to reduce the high cost of health insurance (*what audience does with information*)? Call our toll-free number and get answers today (*information the audience needs*). (*Type of document*—advertisement—and *what document does*—invite—are self-evident.)

A complete purpose statement improves most academic papers. Compare the following two purpose statements:

> This paper compares Hawthorne's character Dimmesdale in *The Scarlet Letter* with Melville's character Claggart in *Billy Budd*. (*What the reader does with the information* is missing, so the document lacks purpose and is less interesting.)
>
> This paper compares Hawthorne's character Dimmesdale in *The Scarlet Letter* with Melville's character Claggart in *Billy Budd*, so one can see the influence that Hawthorne had on Melville. (By

including *what the audience does with the information,* your document has purpose, which adds value.)

Remember, if you partition a document to accommodate multiple audiences, each section of the document needs its own purpose statement:

> Section 1 helps you determine if you are eligible for a student loan.
>
> Section 2 details how eligible students apply for a student loan.

2.4 Use the Purpose Statement to Settle Controversies.

Because the purpose statement defines your document, you want to be certain the purpose statement is correct. Now is the time to find and settle controversies, *before* you invest precious time and effort in a document. If possible, show your purpose statement to colleagues, supervisors—even to the intended audience. Too many writers wait until they finish the document, then discover a fatal flaw. They wrote to the wrong audience, wrote for the wrong purpose, and provided the wrong information. They just wasted their time.

The purpose statement forces people to make firm decisions about the document. Many writers have presented a finished document to a manager who said, "Sorry, that's not what I wanted." They ask, "Can you tell me what you want?" The manager replies, "I'm not sure, but I'll know it when I see it." When confronted with vague requirements, use the analysis techniques to help your manager or client give you concrete and specific guidance about who the audience is and what the audience does with the information.

Managers can review their writers' purpose statements to catch fatal flaws early and ensure that writing assignment instructions are clear. For example, a writer shows the boss a draft purpose statement: *This memo describes the company's pension plan so employees can decide whether to participate.* The boss alters the purpose statement: *This memo explains step by step how employees enroll in the company's pension plan.* The writer just saved hours of writing a document the boss did not want. Also, the boss saved time. Reviewing a purpose statement takes seconds; reviewing the whole document takes much longer.

Similarly, use your purpose statement to get early acceptance from prospective readers, especially clients. The client who accepts your purpose statement is more likely to accept the finished document. Consequently, you write with more confidence and speed.

If you have multiple writers writing sections of a document, make sure each writer understands each other's purpose statement. You avoid overlapping sections, and you identify gaps.

Purpose statements improve the review process, too. When reviewers know the intended audience and what the audience does with the information, they have the context in which to give feedback. Otherwise, each reviewer thinks he or she is the intended audience. Their feedback reflects their point of view, not the intended audience's point of view.

Purpose Statements Make History.

Great documents begin with purpose statements. The following purpose statements helped shape American history. The writers are *can do*, purpose-driven people, the kind of people who make things happen. They know what they want, they know their audience, and they know what the audience must do. They understand completely that their words have consequences. They appeal to reason, not passion. Consider these two documents and how the writers' analysis works to create a purpose statement.

Analysis: In 1787, the second Continental Congress needs to *constitute* a national government *to promote the general welfare and provide for the common defense,* and so forth. The audience is *we the people.* The document name is in the title. The verb *ordain* sets a tone of sacred trust. The Constitution (*type of document*) of the United States of America.

We the People of the United States (*audience and writer*), in Order to form a more perfect Union, establish Justice, insure domestic Tranquility, provide for the common defense, promote the general Welfare, and secure the Blessings of Liberty to ourselves and our Posterity (*what audience does with the information*), do ordain and establish (*what the document does*) this Constitution for the United States of America (*what the audience needs to know*). (Adopted September 17, 1787.)

Analysis: In spring of 1944, General George Patton Jr. needs to organize his new command, the Third Army, in preparations for the allied invasion of Europe, essential to winning World War II. Patton is an excellent communicator, flamboyant in speech but precise on paper. His purpose statement is so precise that you can easily see his analysis.

This letter (*type of document*) will orient (*what the document does*) you, officers of the higher echelons (*audience*), in the principles of command, combat procedure, and administration which obtain in this Army (*what audience needs to know*), and will guide (*more what the document does*) you in the conduct of your several commands (*what audience does with the information*). (General George Patton Jr., March 6, 1944. *The Unknown Patton* by Charles M. Province. Bonanza Books, 1984.)

You find a purpose statement in the Declaration of Independence, Washington's Farewell Address, the Emancipation Proclamation, and many other history-making documents. If you, too, want to make important things happen, begin your document with a purpose statement.

Practice Steps 1 and 2 Using a Case Study.

Use the case study below to practice answering the six analytical questions and assembling a five-part purpose statement.

On April 10, Federal Systems, Inc.'s office manager sent the following two-page memo by e-mail to the facility's 320 employees, and posted the memo by all the elevator doors.

To: Federal Systems, Inc. employees

From: Office Manager

Subject: Spring Maintenance on Parking Lot

As you are aware, last winter was particularly cold. We had many days of freeze and thaw that caused the unsightly cracks in the parking lot asphalt. Now the days are getting longer and warmer: Spring is in the air! With Spring comes the annual maintenance of the parking lot. The building manager needs to seal those cracks before weeds take root and wedge the little cracks into big cracks.

(continued)

(continued)

The maintenance process has two steps. First, they need to clean the parking lot of all debris and grind out and patch damaged asphalt. Then they can apply the sealant. Finally, they repaint the lines.

Consequently, the building manager asked me to inform you that they plan to begin the maintenance next week. Weather permitting, they plan to seal half the lot (the east side) on Monday, April 14, and the other half (the west side) on Wednesday, April 16. The sealant dries in two days. They plan to paint lines on Friday, April 18.

Therefore, only half the parking lot would be available Monday through Thursday. The entire lot will be closed Friday and reopen the next Monday morning.

To ensure that the work proceeds on schedule, the building manager intends to tow cars if necessary to clear the lot. Our lease gives the building manager the option of passing any towing fees to the person towed, who must pay a minimum $110 to retrieve his or her vehicle from the impound lot.

On Monday, the building manager ordered 14 cars towed. The unhappy employees admitted that they did not read the whole memo because it was about cracks and weeds—useless information.

Let's see how analysis and a purpose statement can help us avoid this expensive mess. Use these four techniques:

1. Answer the six analytical questions—one question about yourself as the writer and five questions about the audience.

2. Decide the type of document to use. The communication is internal, so a memo is appropriate. Sending the memo as an e mail is economical, plus you want a record for your files. You can also post the memo on the bulletin board or in the elevators.

3. Pick a verb that describes what the document does. A neutral tone is not strong enough. The document needs to *notify* or *warn* employees.

4. Use your analysis to assemble the five pieces of the purpose statement that you use as the first sentence of the memo.

What result do you want?	*I want the employees to solve their own parking problem next week.*
Who is the audience?	*Employees who drive to work.*
What does the audience do with the information?	*Make other plans and avoid towing.*
What information does the audience need?	*The schedule of parking lot closures.*
Does the audience know little or much about the information?	*They know much about parking.*
Does the audience need proof?	*No, they believe me.*

Even if the employees are impatient and read only the first 26 words—about ten seconds—of the following memo, they have the essential information to avoid towing.

To: Federal Systems employees who drive

From: Office Manager

Subject: Make plans for parking lot closures, April 14–18

This memo notifies employees who drive to work about parking lot closures April 14 through 18. Please make other plans to avoid having your car towed.

Note the schedule of closures. The east side closes for resealing April 14 and 15. The west side closes for resealing April 16 and 17. The entire lot closes for line painting April 18. If you are towed, you pay a minimum $110 towing fee to the impound lot.

Let's all plan ahead to avoid the hassle and expense of having our cars towed.

Select Facts

Use your document's purpose statement to help you select facts. The purpose statement defines what facts are relevant.

Don't confuse facts with information. *Facts* are the evidence we can know by study or experience. *Information* is facts organized to be useful. Later, in Step 4 ("Organize Your Points in a Sentence Outline"), the writer's challenge is to organize *facts* into *information*. However, our present task is to select the facts that we later organize.

You select only the facts the reader needs. In the workplace, having too many facts is as big a problem as having too few. With access to the Internet and a few keystrokes in a search engine, you can bury yourself and your audience in facts, mixing irrelevant and relevant facts. In school, we tried to impress the teacher with how many facts we gathered, proving that our research was thorough. In the workplace, we need to impress our reader by carefully selecting the useful facts—a small subset of the facts we know, a small subset of our research.

Don't confuse *selecting* facts with *researching* facts. For example, in the laboratory, you follow the scientific method. Having observed a phenomenon, you invent a hypothesis and make predictions; you test your hypothesis with experiments or field observations; you modify your hypothesis to conform to the test results; you repeat the process until your hypothesis consistently predicts your test results. At the end of your experiments, you may have file cabinets filled with your notes—mostly facts. However, when you write your document about your experiments, you select only the facts that your reader needs.

Don't confuse *selecting* facts for a document with *gathering* work-related facts. Many work procedures require gathering facts. For example, you use a detailed procedure—a checklist—to inspect a factory for safety hazards. Using the checklist, you gather many pages of facts. However, when you write your report to the factory manager, you select just those facts that the factory manager needs: safety violations and other hazards.

In many jobs, the manager hands the staff worker a checklist to follow: how to inspect the factory, conduct the audit, review the application, design the system, troubleshoot a problem, and so forth. Checklists are excellent tools for gathering facts or performing tasks. However, checklists neither select the facts the reader needs, nor organize the facts the way the reader needs them. Therefore, expecting an author to write a clear, concise, and relevant document strictly following the same checklist is unreasonable.

3.1 Use the Purpose Statement as You Select Facts.

Each part of the purpose statement provides clues to help you select facts. For example, consider selecting facts to support the following purpose statement:

This manual (*type of document*) describes (*what the document does*) to new owners of the Fastcut Lawnmower (*audience*) how to safely operate and properly maintain your new lawnmower (*the information the audience needs* and *what audience does with the information*).

Type of document—*manual*—suggests a set of facts about procedures.

What the document does—*describes*—suggests that we need not *explain* the mechanics or attempt to motivate the new owner.

Select facts that describe *who does what and what does what* with the lawnmower.

Audience—*new owners*—suggests an operator who has no interest in building or repairing small four-cycle engines. Select only practical information about the lawnmower as a tool. Also, the *new owner* probably knows little about lawn mowers, so provide pictures.

Information the audience needs—*how to*—and what the audience does with the information—*safely operate and properly maintain your new lawnmower*—suggest that we limit the facts to instructions about a new lawnmower. Specifically, we need facts on two topics: operations and maintenance. The facts need to be accurate and complete.

Recall that sometimes we must *research* or *gather* facts before we can write our purpose statement. Then, we use the purpose statement as we *select* the facts for the document. For example, after researching ultraviolet rays and skin cancer, I conclude that sunscreens block the rays our bodies use to make vitamin D, a natural defense against cancer. I decide to write an article on my findings. My purpose statement reads: *This paper describes how sunscreens may actually increase the incidence of melanoma so dermatologists can caution patients at risk.* My purpose statement helps me select from my vast notes only those facts relevant to sunscreen, vitamin D, and one type of skin cancer, melanoma. The purpose statement might also help me discover a gap in my facts, requiring more research. For example, can ultraviolet rays change sunscreen into a cancer-causing chemical?

If we can write the purpose statement *before* we conduct our research or fact gathering, we save even more time. The universe of facts is vast. If we can apply the purpose statement's criteria for relevance as we research or gather facts, we can effectively combine research and fact selecting.

4 | Organize Your Points in a Sentence Outline

You finished your analysis of purpose and audience. You have a purpose statement and *facts*. Now use three techniques to select and organize your *points* in a sentence outline:

4.1 Write your points using short words in short sentences.
4.2 Evaluate points to eliminate irrelevancies and redundancies.
4.3 Order the points.

A point is an *opinion* or a *general truth*—not a mere fact. The point organizes the facts, transforming mere facts into useful information. A paragraph is a point supported by facts.

Many writers resist making a point. They are shy about stating an opinion or a general truth; they hope the reader can infer the opinion or general truth from the facts. The reader can't. Some writers think their facts are compelling. Facts are *never* compelling. Smart people draw the wrong conclusions from the right facts every day.

Therefore, you must make a point to tell your audience what the facts mean. Management guru Peter Drucker poses the question, *Do effective managers consider all the facts before making a decision?* The answer is *No*. Effective managers consider all the *opinions of their staff experts* before making a decision. *Do effective staff experts consider all the facts before offering an opinion to the manager?* The answer is *Yes*. However, the staff expert needs to make a point to tell the manager—or any audience—what the facts mean.[1]

Unfortunately, most writers do not outline. Most writers learn outlining in high school, and abandon the technique immediately

---

[1]Peter Drucker, *The Essential Drucker: In One Volume the Best of Sixty Years of Peter Drucker's Essential Writing on Management* (New York: Collins Business, 2001).

upon graduation. Most high school graduates say outlining is a waste of time and effort.

The problem is that most teachers teach outlining the wrong way. They teach you to start with Roman numeral "I." The next level down is capital "A." If you have a capital "A," you must have a capital "B"—some Law of Physics, I suppose. Below the capital "A" comes the Arabic "1," followed by lowercase "a," followed by a parenthetical "(1)," followed by parenthetical "(a)." If the teacher is detail-oriented—and mine was—you follow with lowercase Roman numerals "(iii)," and finally bullets (•). You learn to use between five and eight levels of outlining. Microsoft Word has an automatic out-lining numbering feature that goes to nine levels!

I wrote my high school theme paper about the ancient Romans' feats of engineering. My teacher wanted to approve my outline before I wrote the draft. At the highest level "I," I wrote:

I. *The Romans built roads.*

Next, I needed a capital "A"—something about *how* or *why* the Romans built roads. So I wrote:

A. *They used limestone.*

Then, I needed an Arabic "1," but I didn't know much about limestone, so I went to the family encyclopedia and read about limestone. I chose as my next point:

1. *Limestone is a calcite.*

I now needed a lowercase "a," so I returned to the encyclopedia and dug out another interesting tidbit:

a. *Calcites come from fossil seashells.*

With four more levels to go, I had serious doubts about outlining. I had strayed far from the topic of Roman roads, but I pressed on.

At level "(1)" I hit the Cambrian Explosion; at level "(a)" I stumbled into the Big Bang Theory; at level "(iii)" I was in the mind of God, and I still had another level to go. Like most high school students, I abandoned outlining. I wrote the draft paper first, then backed out the outline to show to my teacher.

Our high school teachers made two fundamental mistakes. They didn't teach us the first four steps of analysis, so we didn't have a way to evaluate our points for relevancy. Plus, they took sentence outlining about six levels too deep.

To write a useful outline, complete the first four steps of analysis before you outline. You need a purpose statement and selected facts to know what points to make. Outline just your points: opinions and general truths. Stay at a high level. *Do not* outline the facts. Outline only the *body* of your document: The *introduction* and *conclusion* follow formats and therefore don't need outlining.

The sentence outline saves much time and effort for writers, reviewers, and readers. As the writer, you can show your sentence outline to reviewers to find irrelevant, redundant, out-of-order, or even missing points. Finding and fixing problems in an outline is faster than finding and fixing the problems in draft paragraphs. With confidence in your outline, you compose the draft faster.

The sentence outline ensures that your document is easier to read. Your points appear at the beginning of paragraphs. Readers skim documents by reading the first sentence of each paragraph. Because your points are simple sentences, they are easy to understand and remember.

4.1 Write Your Points Using Short Words in Short Sentences.

Write your points with short words in simple 3 to 10 word sentences. Long sentences tend to express more than one point, and we want one point for each paragraph. For example, *Monohull boats are more seaworthy, but catamarans are faster.* Is the paragraph about seaworthy monohulls or fast catamarans?

Write your points with the first words that come to mind. Relax—don't worry about supporting your point with facts yet.

This technique is simple when you can distinguish between a *point* and a *fact*. Points have four characteristics that distinguish them from facts.

First, a point is either an *opinion* or a *general truth*. For example, *The costs outweigh the benefits* is an opinion. The supporting facts prove high costs and low benefits. On the other hand, *The costs are both fixed and variable* is a general truth that needs no proof but does need details to specify the fixed and variable costs. *Direct labor is a variable cost* is a fact.

Sometimes, whether your point is an opinion or a general truth is contextual. For example, in high school when I first read, *The speed of light is constant*, I thought I was reading opinion. Later, in college, the constant speed of light was a general truth supported by experimental evidence or facts. Now, the bimetric scalar-tensor gravitational theory says the speed of light varies—back to opinion. Don't worry. As long as you begin your paragraph with your point and follow with the supporting details, your document works. A recommendation is always an opinion. A conclusion is usually a general truth.

Second, points turn facts into useable information. Here are two facts: Bob earns $500 per week waiting tables; the Mercedes E-Class costs $84,500. What is the point? How do we use these facts? The point is *Bob cannot afford a Mercedes E-Class*, a useful opinion based on the facts.

Third, your point—*opinion or general truth*—is usually easier to understand than the supporting facts. For example, the point *"Houston, we have a problem"* is easier to understand than the supporting facts, *"We've had a main B bus undervolt...."*

Fourth, although occasionally a point can stand on its own—such as *gravity works*—most points need supporting facts to help or convince the reader.

Many writers are shy about making a point, especially when the point is an opinion. Consequently, they omit the point or hide it in the middle or end of the paragraph. Sometimes writers think they need to lead the reader through the facts to the point. Don't be shy. The reader needs to see your point—especially your opinion—at the beginning of the paragraph. Supporting facts follow.

4.2 Evaluate Points to Eliminate Irrelevancies and Redundancies.

After you write your points, compare your points to your purpose statement to eliminate irrelevancies. Remember, your purpose statement defines relevancy for the document. If a point does not support your purpose statement, the reader doesn't need the point—it is irrelevant.

If you have a multiple audience, you have multiple purpose statements. You must evaluate your points for each purpose statement. Remember that recommendations and conclusions are always relevant points that you make in the body of the document.

Next, take a second look at any leftover points that you think are irrelevant. They may have value. When subject-matter experts think of points, they are not hallucinating. Consider leftover points four ways:

1. The leftover point is irrelevant to the reader. Eliminate it.
2. The leftover point is really a fact that does not get its own paragraph but belongs under a point in another paragraph.
3. The leftover point may have another audience that you overlooked during analysis. You need to decide if and how you accommodate the additional audience.

4. The leftover point is irrelevant to the reader's purpose for reading, but you want to make the point anyway given your purpose for writing—a perfectly legitimate decision. You can put the irrelevant point in the introduction or conclusion of your document.

For example, in a business letter the reader does not need to know that *I enjoyed meeting you at the Amelia Island conference.* However, you want to make the point anyway to maintain good will. Put the point in the introduction. Keep the body of your document just information the reader needs.

After eliminating irrelevant points from the outline, reread them to eliminate redundancies. If two points need the same supporting facts, the two points are most likely redundant.

If you work with a team of writers, outlining helps you coordinate. Together, you eliminate irrelevancies using the criteria of the agreed-upon purpose statement. Also, you eliminate redundancies before a teammate invests hours writing and editing text. During outlining, irrelevant points are easy to let go because they are a small investment in time—maybe a minute each. Paragraphs that represent hours of work are harder to let go.

4.3 Order the Points.

Order your points the way the reader needs to use them. Look to your analysis for two valuable clues.

The first clue is what the audience does with the information. Recall that audiences do three things with information:

1. The audience who gives advice needs to master your information. They want the points organized as *sources and methods,* then *findings,* then *conclusion* or *recommendation.* They need to follow the steps of your logical process leading to your conclusion or recommendation.

2. The audience who uses your information to make decisions or plans wants the *conclusion or recommendation* first, then the *findings*. Omit or limit sources and methods. Decision makers hire experts who consider sources and methods.
3. The audience who uses your information to perform a task wants *the expected result,* then *instructions how to achieve the result.* They do not need the sources and methods.

You get a second clue if your purpose statement includes a list of topics that the audience needs to know. You make your points in the same order that you list the topics:

This proposal describes *our qualifications, technical approach, costs, and your savings* if we convert your telephone system to wireless.

In this example, the first points are about *qualifications.* The second set of points is about the *technical approach*, and so on.

In addition to using the two clues, put yourself in the reader's place. Rarely does the reader want to see the information in the same order that you gathered it. Here's a simple example. I prepare a grocery list for my teenage daughter. I gather my information working clockwise around my kitchen. First, I check the freezer: ice cream, frozen vegetables. Next, I check the refrigerator: milk, deli meats, fresh vegetables, and condiments. Finally, I work through the cabinets checking the dry goods: cereal, coffee, tea, flour, sugar, and spices. The grocery store organization is not like my kitchen. To make the list work for my daughter, I need to rearrange my list to match the layout of the store: fruits and vegetables first, then deli, then bakery, dry goods, dairy, and frozen foods last.

For another example, suppose you inspect a manufacturing plant for safety, working spatially from front to back of the plant, taking notes as you go. However, the reader wants your report organized topically—first, safety violations in the facility, then safety violations in the equipment, and finally, safety violations in procedures.

Take advantage of standard formats. Often organizations have standard documents such as contracts, appraisals, staff studies, meeting minutes, trip reports, and policies. Writers in the organization already worked through the analysis for your writing situation. They determined how to partition the document into sections according to the audiences. They determined the broad topics that the audiences need to know, and they put those topics in order. Their analysis incorporated in the standard format saves you some time and effort.

Although formats are the fruits of other's successful analysis, a format is no substitute for doing your own analysis. Formats do not determine the points or the facts, just the order of the topics. Within the topics, you still need to select facts, determine the points, check points for relevancy and redundancy, and put points in order.

Don't deviate from your organization's standard formats. The familiar format helps your readers know what to expect and how to use the document.

Some common formats follow:

Document	Topics
Proposal	Executive summary, technical approach, management plan, past experience, costs.
Business Plan	Strategy and organization, product, marketing, physical plant, personnel, accounting controls, capital requirements; appendices for pro forma income statements, balance sheet, cashflow.
Agenda	Old business, new business.
Staff Study	Problem, solution, facts, discussion.

Make sure the order of your points works *before* you compose your draft. Putting whole paragraphs in order takes more time than putting points in order.

Practice Steps 1 through 4 Using a Case Study.

The following case study is true; we changed the names. Use this case to practice all four steps in analysis.

What Happened

Universe Bank hired ACME Systems, Inc. to build a new system to process merchant credit card transactions. The contract requires deploying the new system on February 20 when retail sales are seasonally slowest. Then ACME has 45 days to fix problems in the software. In October, 18 months into the contract and four months before the planned deployment, ACME showed the Universe Bank president a demo of the system. The president was so pleased that he requested that ACME accelerate deploying the new credit card system before Thanksgiving. He estimates the bank might save $360,000 by accelerating deployment.

The president's request stunned ACME's project manager and software engineers. They thought, "The bank president no longer *believes* that we need to deploy in February when retail sales volume is low. He doesn't believe us because he *knows*

(continued)

(continued)

little about project management and systems engineering. Therefore, he needs all the *information* we know about project management and systems engineering."

The bank's Information Technology (IT) manager agreed with ACME that acceleration is risky. The IT manager suggested that ACME write a paper to the bank president to change his mind.

The ACME project manager and three senior engineers worked nights and the weekend to produce a gorgeous 40-page, four-color document for the bank president. The document explains how accelerating deployment of the credit card system *"violated the best practices of the life-cycle management of large systems integration projects . . . specifically, late-term acceleration contradicted the Synergism-Catalist ISO 9000 methodology bid in the risk mitigation plan. . . ."*

The 40-page document failed. Six hours after ACME submitted their masterpiece to the bank president, ACME got an answer. The president returned the document with a note scrawled in fountain pen ink on the cover, *"That's why we hired you geniuses. Make it happen!"*

ACME Systems' analysis was fatally flawed. They did not focus on the key part of the analysis, *what the audience—the bank president—does with information.* Instead, they began their analysis assuming the president didn't believe them and therefore needed proof. If you do not perform analysis in the right order, you almost always write the wrong document. In this case, the 40-page document was full of detailed proofs to thrill any project manager—all irrelevant to a bank president.

Let's use the *Can Do Writing* system to fix this failed communication.

Step 1: We begin by analyzing the two potential audiences.

What do you want?	We want to keep the original contract deployment	
Who is the audience?	*Universe Bank president*	*IT manager*
What does the audience do with the information?	*Decide whether to accelerate deployment*	*Advise senior bank management*
What information does the audience need?	*Business risks*	*Technical risks*
Does audience know little or much?	*Knows much about business*	*Knows much about technology*
Does audience believe you or need proof?	*Wants proof*	*Believes*

We need to use judgment to decide how to partition the information for the two audiences.

Step 2: We write a purpose statement for each audience. We decide to write a technical report to the IT manager and a letter to the bank president. However, the president wants proof, and the proof is in the facts about the technical risks. Whereas the bank president knows much about business risks, he knows little about technical risks. Even though the president knows little about the technology, we decide to attach the Technical Report to the letter. The Technical Report includes the proofs we provide the IT manager, who in turn can advise the president on technology.

The last part of our purpose statement is the verb. We think the acceleration is a serious enough problem that we pick the verb *warns* to set the tone:

> This letter warns you about the business risks if you decide to accelerate deploying the credit card system.

For the Technical Report's purpose statement, we pick a verb that ensures that the reader expects much detail. Note how the purpose statement helps both the IT manager and the bank president:

> This Technical Report details the technical risks of accelerating deployment of the credit card system so the IT manager can advise senior bank management.

When the bank president goes to the attachment of the letter looking for proof, the purpose statement sets expectations. *Technical Report*—the president reads financial reports, not technical reports. *Details*—the president considers big issues; the staff handles details. *Technical risks*—the president knows he personally lacks technical expertise; he can't reset his password on his computer. *IT manager*—the president instantly realizes that he has a staff expert who knows this technology. *Advise senior bank management*—now the president knows that if he wants proof, he can call his trusted IT manager for advice.

Step 3: We select the facts that the bank president and the IT manager need for their respective documents. These facts include estimates of system down time and lost transaction revenue, and problems with customer service. We have many facts about the difficulty of integrating the system with the 17,000 merchants and their assortment of card readers. We need more staff to accelerate deployment.

Step 4: We organize our points into outlines. We start by writing our points:

Acceleration puts your customers at risk during their busiest season.

We are on schedule and in budget for the February 20 delivery.

We need 45 days after deployment to ensure system stability.

An unstable system may be off-line three hours per day.

ACME must assign four additional engineers to accelerate deployment.

We cannot anticipate all the integration problems from the 17,000 customers accessing the new system.

Some larger customers' systems are custom-built and poorly documented.

Acceleration may cause a loss of $1.3 million in revenue.

You might lose customers.

The bank's reputation might suffer.

ACME's reputation may suffer if the accelerated system fails.

We recommend you keep the original contract schedule.

To accelerate, we must modify the contract and increase our fees.

The following six points are relevant for the bank president:

1. Acceleration puts your customers at risk during their busiest season.
2. Acceleration may cause a loss of $1.3 million in revenue.
3. You might lose customers.
4. The bank's reputation might suffer.
5. We recommend you keep the original contract schedule.
6. To accelerate, we must modify the contract and increase our fees.

The following five points are relevant for the IT manager:

1. We need 45 days after deployment to ensure system stability.
2. An unstable system may be off-line 3 hours per day.
3. We cannot anticipate all the integration problems from the 17,000 customers accessing the new system.
4. Some larger customers' systems are custom-built and poorly documented.
5. We recommend you keep the original contract schedule.

Note: Some points for the IT manager might also be supporting facts in paragraphs for the letter to the president. For example, the IT manager needs a whole paragraph explaining how you determine that *the unstable system can be off-line 3 hours per day*. You might use the same sentence as a fact to support your point that *acceleration may cause a loss of $1.3 million*.

Three points are irrelevant to both the president and the IT manager:

1. *We are on schedule and in budget for the February 20 delivery* is not a business risk caused by acceleration; however, we may want to make this point anyway by putting it in the introduction.
2. *ACME's reputation may suffer if the accelerated system fails* is irrelevant to the bank; however, you might use this point in a memo to ACME management.
3. *ACME must assign four additional engineers* is a fact that supports the point to the president about changing the contract and increasing fees.

Two points in the letter to the president are redundant. The sentence about putting customers at risk during their busy season is really a fact that supports the point that *the bank might lose customers.* Two points to the IT manager are redundant. The sentence about customers having custom-built, poorly documented systems is really a fact supporting the point, *we can't anticipate all the integration problems.*

Finally, we put the points in order. The letter to the president begins with the recommendation because the president reads to make a decision:

> We recommend you keep the original contract schedule.
> Acceleration may cause a loss of $1.3 million in revenue.
> You might lose customers.
> The bank's reputation might suffer.
> To accelerate, we must modify the contract and increase our fees.

The Technical Report has the recommendation at the end because the IT manager reads to master the subject matter and give advice:

> We cannot anticipate all the integration problems from the 17,000 customers accessing the new system.
> We need 45 days after deployment to ensure system stability.
> An unstable system may be off-line three hours per day.
> We recommend you keep the original contract schedule.

End of the Story

For their second attempt to communicate with the bank president, ACME performed the analysis in the right order and produced a one-page letter using the purpose statement and outline. The bank president was able to skim the letter and quickly decide to keep the original contract schedule. In February, the integration problems were severe, but credit card volume was so low that the bank customers did not notice.

Skillset: Composing the Draft

When I have nothing to say, my lips are sealed.
—Talking Heads, "Psycho Killer"

There is no such thing as *writers' block*—only analysts' block. If you find yourself staring at the computer screen, you are either too tired to write, or you don't know what to say. You have not forgotten how to talk. Saying nothing is the mature response when you don't know what to say. (Ironically, most people who announce, *I'm speechless*, continue talking.)

If you don't know what to say, you need to work backward through analysis to find the problem. Perhaps your point is irrelevant. Perhaps you need to gather and select facts. Perhaps your purpose statement is wrong. Perhaps you lost sight of your audience and the information they need.

If your analysis is sound, you know what to say. If you know what to say, you can write your draft because language is instinct, hard-wired into your amazing brain. We started learning language as babies. A typical high school student has a working vocabulary between 36,000 and 60,000 words. Shakespeare, in all of his works, used 20,138 base words. When someone says, *I'm at a loss for words*, they really mean, *I don't know what to say*. They have plenty of words. The problem is that they did not do the analysis.

Use your language instinct. Don't let words become an impediment to writing your draft. Never have a dictionary open on your desk as you write your draft. Never use a thesaurus when you write your draft. Keep your language simple. Don't let grammar become an impediment when writing your draft. You use adequate grammar when you speak—not perfect, but good enough to write a draft. Later, you fix errors in word choice, grammar, punctuation, and mechanics.

Put yourself in a good environment—quiet, well lit, and comfortable. Let the answering machine take your phone calls for a couple of hours. You can tolerate interruptions during analysis and editing, but not while you write your draft.

Remove distractions. Manage the settings on your word processor. Turn off the feature that checks spelling and grammar while you type—a distraction. Turn off autocorrect features that get in your way. For example, my word processor attempts to autocorrect typos. I dropped the letter *s* when typing *lessons learned*. The machine autocorrected my text to *lesions learned*. Because the wrong word was spelled correctly, I didn't see the mistake when I ran my spell-checker. Ouch.

Compose the Draft

After you finish analysis, turn on your word processor and compose the draft. Transcribe your purpose statement and your sentence outline into your word processor. Your purpose statement becomes the first sentence in your introduction. The points in your sentence outline become the first sentences in your paragraphs.

All documents present information in the following order: introduction, body, and conclusion. Each part of the document serves a different purpose. The introduction helps readers use the document. The body provides the information readers need. The conclusion tells readers what happens next.

However, you compose your draft in the order of these five techniques:

5.1 Compose the draft body.
5.2 Compose the draft conclusion.
5.3 Compose the draft introduction.
5.4 If necessary, compose the draft executive summary.
5.5 If necessary, compose the informative abstract.

Most writers get the order wrong, composing the introduction first—a linear approach. However, the introduction introduces the *document*. Until you have the body and the conclusion, you don't have a document to introduce. You don't really know what you need to put in the introduction. When composed first, introductions are usually too long and full of irrelevant information. Many people use writing the introduction as a substitute for analysis; consequently, their introduction includes information that belongs in the body or in an executive summary.

Some documents, if necessary, use an executive summary or an abstract to help a secondary audience. Therefore, the executive summary and abstract are optional. Each performs a different purpose. A person reads an executive summary, having decided *not* to read the underlying document. A person reads an abstract to decide *whether* to read the underlying document.

Conclusions, introductions, executive summaries, and abstracts have different formulas. We describe each formula in this step.

5.1 Compose the Draft Body.

Use these four tips as you compose your draft:

1. Compose paragraphs by adding facts to support each point in your sentence outline. You can cut facts later when you have the whole picture. Usually, you need no more than five sentences to support a point.
2. Compose with the first words that come to mind, using simple *who does what* and *what does what* sentences.
3. Postpone fact, format, word, grammar, punctuation, and mechanics problems. Use brackets to mark [questionable words or facts]. Put [questions to yourself or colleagues] in brackets. Don't let small details distract you. After you compose the draft, you fix any problems in the brackets.
4. Take short ten-minute breaks every hour. Professional writers can compose about 45 to 50 minutes before they get tired—mentally tired. Also, professional writers compose draft for two or three hours per day.

Composing with an outline saves time. First, you write with confidence. Second, if you have an outline, you can return from breaks and efficiently resume composing the draft beginning with the next point in your outline. If you do not have an outline, you most likely reread your draft to recollect your train of thought. Moreover, if you are like 99 percent of writers, you cannot resist editing as you reread your draft. Premature editing can double the time to produce a document.

A document composed from an outline is easier to read. With the points at the beginning of the paragraph, the reader can efficiently skim read your document. Corporations invest millions of dollars trying to pack big ideas into short, easy-to-remember sentences.

Outlines make documents more persuasive. Your paragraphs begin with short and therefore easy-to-remember points. Easy-to-remember points are more persuasive than longer, hard-to-remember points.

Emphasize key points and facts in short sentences, as short as six words. People remember short sentences and forget long ones. Develop complex facts with longer sentences inside the paragraph. Use vertical lists to group logically related items, statements, commands, or questions.

Don't worry about finding the *perfect* words or phrases. *Perfect* wording is usually a matter of personal preference. Plus, you will have a better idea of the best word choice after you complete the draft. Remember to use simple words. If you are the only person in the room who knows the word, why use it? Readers resent unnecessary trips to the dictionary.

5.2 Compose the Draft Conclusion.

For most documents, the conclusion is a simple formula: Tell the reader *what happens next* or *who does what next*. Examples include:

- Please call if you have any questions.
- I'll call you in a week to answer any questions you may have.
- We look forward to working with you.
- After you approve this general design, we can begin writing the detailed specifications.
- By using your "My Account" software, you can start saving money today.

Your conclusion—*what happens next*—usually recalls the purpose statement, specifically the outcome or what the audience does with the information. For example, the purpose statement reads: *This message informs you of my itinerary so we can schedule a meeting.* The conclusion recalls the purpose statement: *Please inform me by return e-mail the time and place of the meeting.*

Make your conclusion as specific as possible. The expression, *Your help in any way is much appreciated . . .* begs to be ignored. Instead write, *Please correct my account and send me an accurate Form 1099 before January 30.*

In academic writing, the paper's conclusion is often a different formula: a summary of key findings. However, in business and technical documents, any summary of key findings goes in the executive summary that we describe later.

5.3 Compose the Draft Introduction.

All documents need an introduction. The function of the introduction is to help the reader use the document. You cannot really know what help the reader needs in the introduction until you finish your analysis and compose the body and conclusion. If you try to compose the introduction first, you are trying to introduce something that does not exist yet—an exercise in frustration.

The introduction is a formula with two mandatory parts and five optional parts. We discuss each in turn.

The two mandatory parts of the introduction are:

1. Purpose statement.
2. Plan of the document.

Purpose statement. Focus your reader by putting the purpose statement at the beginning of the introduction. The purpose statement immediately gets to the point of the communication. You will never be accused of *beating around the bush* if you use a purpose statement. Consider the following purpose statement and how it helps the reader:

> This letter alerts horse owners about the dangers of the recent outbreak of the West Nile virus and how to protect your horse by inoculation.

This 24 word purpose statement is full of useful information, helping me, the reader, four ways. First, I know that I have a *letter* in my hands—typically a short communication. Second, if I am not a *horse owner*, I can stop reading after four words. I already get the sense that this writer will not waste my time. However, I do own a horse, so I read on. Third, the word *alerts* sets the tone—this letter has serious consequences. Fourth, I am going to read about three *topics*: the recent West Nile outbreak, why it is dangerous to horses, and inoculations. My *purpose* for reading is to protect my beloved horse.

Plan of the document. Readers need to learn about the plan of your document for two reasons. First, when readers know the plan of the document, they can focus all their attention on your points and supporting facts. Without a plan, readers get distracted, wondering how points and facts relate. Second, readers can use the plan to find information of particular interest. Sometimes the purpose statement incorporates the plan. For example, the purpose statement about West Nile virus presents three topics in order: the recent West Nile outbreak, why it is dangerous to horses, and inoculations.

If your purpose statement adequately states the plan, don't repeat it. For example: *This safety audit report describes problems with your equipment and procedures that you need to fix so you can lower your insurance premiums.* The phrase *problems with equipment and procedures* serves as the document plan.

This next example needs a second sentence to describe the plan: *This pamphlet explains how college students can apply for a First Thrift auto loan. You learn about eligibility, insurance requirements, rates, and responsibilities.*

Having committed to the plan of the document in writing, make sure you follow the plan. You can use the key words in the plan for subheads in your document. For example, the *auto loan pamphlet* can use four subheads: *Eligibility, Insurance Requirements, Rates,* and *Responsibilities.* The combination of plan of document plus subheads helps readers use the pamphlet.

If your audience already knows much about the information and does not require proof, you can often limit your introduction to just the purpose statement and plan of the document. Many shorter documents such as e-mails, memos, or sections of documents need just one-sentence introductions.

The five optional parts of the introduction are:

1. Background.
2. Audience.
3. Sources and methods.
4. Key words.
5. Limitations.

When writing background-through-limitations, you don't follow any particular order, although typically background comes immediately after the plan of the document. Also, you don't need to treat each part as a separate paragraph.

Background helps the reader put the needed information in context. In the background, you discuss the underlying work, significance, or situation addressed by the information in the body. Limit the background to information the reader needs to use the document.

Many writers make the mistake of beginning documents with background. However, background—perhaps fascinating—is irrelevant until the reader knows the critical information in the purpose statement.

The background is also a useful place to make a point irrelevant to the body, but a point you want to make anyway. For example, in a sales letter you make this irrelevant but charming point in the introduction: *I thoroughly enjoyed visiting your delightful city. Omaha is lovely!*

Audience as described in the purpose statement is usually sufficient. However, you can use the introduction to provide further details or make assumptions about the audience: *In this manual we assume the user has a working knowledge of cost accounting and is familiar with IRS Form 5500 EZ.*

Sources and methods help the readers quickly learn where you got the information that they need. In few words, tell the readers that you *researched the literature, performed experiments, consulted a survey,* or *referred to other documents.* You may devote a whole section of the body of your document to sources and methods later. Do not begin your letters, *This letter is in reference to . . .* (perhaps the weakest way to begin correspondence). The cited reference is a source appropriate *after* the purpose statement.

Keywords might need definitions to help the reader with unfamiliar words, concepts, and jargon. For example: *In this policy, part-time employee refers to persons who work fewer than 32 hours each week.* Don't put a glossary in the introduction: A glossary or list of acronyms comes after the main document. You can also define how you use visual devices in the document. For example, *Safety warnings are in a black border box.*

Limitations are practical realities to manage, not ignore. If you have a limitation to your document or your argument, acknowledge the limitation in the introduction. Sometimes the limitation is in the research: *Although we conducted 250 interviews of veterinarians, we do not have results from clinical trials.* Sometimes the limitation is the document itself: *This manual does not describe installation of any third-party devices to your computer.* Readers who discover unacknowledged limitations in the body or conclusion become suspicious—*what else is the author hiding?*

Do not put your recommendation or need-to-know points in the introduction. They belong in the body and executive summary.

Beware of poor template introductions with headings such as *Purpose* and *Scope.* You need to ask, "purpose and scope of *what?*" Purpose or scope of the *work* equals background: *The purpose of the new Visa Card system is to improve Universe Bank's commercial services. The scope of the project involves phases to design, build, test, install, and debug.*

Purpose of the *document* equals our purpose statement and scope of the *document* equals our plan of the document: *This letter warns you about the business risks if you decide to accelerate deploying the credit card system. We discuss three business risks: lost revenue, lost customers, and damaged reputation.* If you must work with a poor template, try to put the purpose and scope of the document first—purpose statement and plan. Then treat the purpose and scope of the work as background.

We note two exceptions to the introduction's formula. First, some scientific academic journals put the purpose statement and plan of the document at the *end* of the introduction. Follow the formula mandated by the editor.

The second exception is when you must communicate bad news. The purpose statement might be overly blunt. Instead, use the following formula. Begin with a short, noncontroversial statement: *Last year the core inflation rate increased 3.5 percent while our energy costs increased 12.8 percent.* Immediately follow with a purpose statement: *Therefore, this letter notifies you that effective March 1, your condo fee increases 7.25 percent.*

The following example of an introduction shows all seven parts:

Report of the National Commission of Writing[2]

This report describes the growing gap between business's need for employees with writing skills and the writing skills of college graduates. Leaders in government, business, and education need to consider ways to narrow this gap.

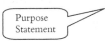

First, we report findings that measure the gap for manufacturing and service industries. Second, we measure industry's investment in closing the gap. In Appendix A, the National Commission on Writing recommends policies to narrow the gap.

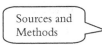

The College Entrance Examination Board, Inc. commissioned a survey of 120 major corporations employing 8 million people. The survey responds to a growing concern about the decline in writing skills as the economy moves forward into the Information Age.

Throughout the report, we make a distinction between hourly and professional employees. We define an hourly employee as eligible for overtime pay.

---

[2]Adapted from *Writing: A Ticket to Work or a Ticket Out* (National Commission on Writing for America's Families, Schools, and Colleges, September 2004).

The data for the manufacturing sector includes all heavy and light manufacturing. However, the data on the services industry is limited to financial, insurance, and real estate corporations.

5.4 If Necessary, Compose the Draft Executive Summary.

Managers often do not have time to read a long document. They want to read a summary instead. The executive summary comes before the introduction and serves managers by highlighting the information for making decisions and plans:

1. Purpose statement.
2. Recommendation.
3. Key points.
4. What happens next (optional).

Actually, you have already written the parts of the executive summary. Look at your outline: You have a purpose statement, a recommendation, and the key points. Your conclusion already states *what happens next*. All you need to do is reassemble these parts, eliminate points that do not concern the manager, and decide if you want to include the *what happens next*. For example, recall the exercise about the letter to the Universe Bank president. The same outline can become an executive summary:

Executive Summary

This letter warns Bank Management about the business risks of accelerating deploying the credit card system. We recommend you keep the original contract schedule. Acceleration may cause a loss of $1.3 million in revenue. The bank might lose customers and the bank's reputation might suffer. To accelerate, ACME must modify the contract and increase fees.

Consequently, your executive summary repeats the key points in your main document, usually word for word. This repetition is good. An executive summary that deviates from the main document is misleading because it gives managers a different set of points.

Summaries are short: one-half to one page. Usually, the purpose statement, recommendation, and *what happens next* are each one sentence long. The number of key points varies. Select the key points from your outline that concern the manager. Resist adding comments or supporting details. The manager can read the main document for those details. Use words that the manager knows. Avoid technical jargon.

Don't mix formulas in your executive summary. Specifically, don't add background and other elements from the introduction.

Note one exception: Large proposals often have a section titled "Executive Summary" much longer than the short formula we describe. In a proposal, the executive summary section acts like a *digest*, restating the key points *plus* the most important supporting facts.

5.5 If Necessary, Compose the Draft Abstract.

Experts read abstracts to decide whether they want to invest time reading the whole document. An abstract has five parts that give the expert enough information to decide:

1. Topic—what did we study?
2. Significance of the topic—why did we study it?
3. Sources and methods—how did we study it?

4. Key points—what findings did we learn?

5. Conclusion—what can we conclude from the findings?

Abstracts are short, rarely longer than one-half of a page. Note that the order of the abstract is the same used for the audience who gives advice. Also, note that the abstract and executive summaries both have key points. However, abstracts use technical language and assume knowledge of advanced concepts, whereas executive summaries use simpler language.

Don't mix formats. Specifically, don't include background or other parts of the introduction. Don't add supporting facts. The reader can find those facts in the document.

For example, recall the exercise about the Technical Report to the Universe Bank IT manager. Note how the following abstract addresses the expert who gives advice rather than the manager who makes decisions.

Abstract

A team of ACME senior engineers examined the technical risks of accelerating deployment of the Universe Bank Visa Card™ credit card processing system. If the system fails to meet functional requirements, the bank may experience serious financial consequences. The team ran test simulations and sensitivity analysis to identify weaknesses in the system in its present state of development. The simulations indicate that the system may be off-line three hours per day. Moreover, an untested system may operate at less than 50 percent efficiency. Moreover, the simulations cannot account for all the possible integration problems from the bank's 17,000 customers' old, poorly documented legacy systems. The team believes it still needs 45 days after deployment to ensure system stability. Therefore, the team concludes that acceleration involves a high degree of technical risk.

Skillset: Editing

Good prose is like a window pane.

— George Orwell

Good text, like a window pane, is transparent so the reader can clearly see the content. Therefore, good editing makes the text clear. Bad editing obscures the text and the content. When we write for our jobs, any edit intended to display the author's personal *style* detracts from the content and is counterproductive.

Edit systematically. You get better results in less time. First, we edit by reviewing the document to ensure the logic. Second, we apply verbal and visual clues to make the logic more obvious to the reader. Then we edit to make the sentences clear, concise, and easy to read.

Compared to analysis and writing, editing is easy. Analysis involves some creative problem solving, and composing involves the hard work of recording points and facts. Editing is more mechanical—a set of logical tests and techniques you apply to your document. You do not need to be a grammar expert to perform these edits. For most of the edits, you need to recognize simple word patterns.

Plan your time and be practical. The editing phase is usually 50 percent of the work. However, some documents deserve a more thorough edit. The use-once-throw-away e-mail does not deserve the same thorough edit as your resume.

You are the best person to edit your document. You did the analysis. Therefore, you know the information your audience needs. If a sentence is unclear, you know best the point or fact you want to communicate. Also, you know best if you can cut a word without changing your meaning.

Edit systematically. Perform the edits in the order we present them. Editing is a multipass activity; focus on one or two techniques per pass. Don't get fixated on any particular sentence. If you can't fix the problem quickly, move on. Writing is an earned skill, and you improve with each document. The problem you struggle with today becomes easy in time.

For longer documents, we recommend you edit from paper. Why? First, the word processor lets you see just a small window of your document, like having blinders on. You can't see problems with consistency. Second, people read about 25 percent faster on paper than they do on screen. For the same reason, people edit about 25 percent faster on paper. For short e-mails, we don't print, mark copy, and transcribe edits, but for longer documents we do. Typically, if the document exceeds two pages, you edit faster on paper.

Review the Draft for Organization and Logic

Review your draft for its organization and logic to make sure that you do not waste time editing a fatally flawed document. Use these three techniques:

6.1 Test organization by answering three questions.
6.2 Use sentence outlining techniques to improve organization.
6.3 Test logic by answering five questions.

If you followed the analytical steps so far, your document most likely has good organization and logic. Nevertheless, review the draft to make sure. A review requires a quick read through the document and is worth the effort.

Also, you can use the three organization and five logic questions to review other authors' documents. Because you know the techniques in analysis, you can suggest specific techniques to correct specific errors. With rare exceptions, poorly organized documents have the same cause: The author either skipped or took shortcuts in analysis.

Time spent repairing errors can range from several hours per page to a couple of minutes per page depending on the type of error. Repairing organization errors may require hours per page because you must go back to analysis. You need to use sentence-outlining techniques to carefully extract and analyze the points to determine relevance, put the points in order, and recompose the draft. On the other hand, repairing most logical errors takes little time—minutes per page. Errors in fact involve a few minutes gathering more information.

Review the draft *before* you edit for coherence or style. Editing a document that has organization or logic problems wastes time and effort. You might spend hours editing your draft for coherence, clarity, economy, and readability and then discover that the points are irrelevant, the facts are wrong, or the organization is unworkable.

6.1 Test Organization by Answering Three Questions.

Ensure that your document presents the information organized in a way that helps the audience. Using a sentence outline practically guarantees that your document has good organization.

If you answer *yes* to any of these three questions, your document fails the organization test:

1. Do your paragraphs begin with facts?
2. Does the document read like a story?
3. Is the document filled with *I, me,* and *mine?*

The organization test is a troubleshooting guide. If you answer *no* to all the questions, your document is organized—maybe not in the *best* way, but good enough.

If your paragraphs begin with facts, we are most likely reading your notes from your research. You have what many call a *data dump.* Your reader rarely wants to read your notes: *The door panels are quarter-inch thick stainless steel. Orthogonal, notched, mechanically interlocked stainless steel stiffeners separate the two panels. Autogeneous welds fasten the stiffeners to the panels.* The reader needs to know what the series of facts means. The reader wants you to organize your data under your points, either opinion or general truth: *Using panels separated with stiffeners makes a watertight door 27 percent lighter than the standard Navy watertight door.*

If your document reads like a story, we are most likely reading how you solved the problem or how the information affects you: *We received your order for three books. The warehouse checked the inventory. They informed operations that they had only two books left. Operations prepared an order for another printing.* Readers rarely want to know how you solve your problems; rather, readers want the information in the order that helps them: *Your book order ships in four weeks.*

If your document is full of *I, me, mine,* you lack a sense of audience. You wrote your draft from your point of view—how the circumstances affect you, rather than how the circumstances affect the audience who uses the information in the document. The words *I, me,* and *mine* are fine, if balanced with *you* and *yours.*

If your document lacks organization, you need to revisit analysis in the next section—"Use Sentence Outlining Techniques to Improve Organization." If your document passes the organization test, you can skip to the section, "Test Logic by Answering Five Questions."

6.2 Use Sentence Outlining Techniques to Improve Organization.

If the document lacks organization, go back to sentence outlining. Treat your poorly organized document as research notes. You can select points and facts from the document and reuse them.

Use these five sentence outlining techniques to improve the document's organization:

1. Pull points from the paragraphs—opinions and general truths—and compose them as short sentences.
2. Write a purpose statement after analyzing audience and purpose.

3. Compare the points against your purpose statement to eliminate irrelevancies and redundancies.
4. Add points you think are missing.
5. Order the points the way the audience wants to see the
   information.

After you craft a sentence outline, you rewrite the draft. You are
lucky if you can use 20 percent of the former draft.

Here are some clues to help you find the points. Look near the
end of the paragraph. Many authors list their facts, then conclude
with their point. Look for words like *Therefore* or *It should be noted*
within the paragraph. Authors often instinctively draw attention to
the point. If the paragraph is a string of facts without a point, you
need to ask, *What point, if any, was the author trying to make with these
facts?*

In this paragraph about a kitchen health inspection, we mark the
point in italics:

Table surfaces were dirty. Walls had a sticky film of grease. The
steam kettles had a ring of putrefied brown gravy. The grease in
the deep-fat fryer was at least two weeks old. The refrigerator
was too full and four degrees too warm. Many food containers
indicated the contents were past the expiration date. *These
deficiencies alone warrant closing your restaurant.* The tile grout on
the floors was green with algae.

Often our writing assignment is a response to an earlier document. For example, we may answer correspondence, or we may
write the general design from the functional description. Do not
automatically mimic the organization of the earlier document. Why?

First, the earlier document may have poor organization. Second, the earlier document's organization might be good for its audience but inappropriate for your document's audience.

Review the earlier document. Then if necessary, pull the points, evaluate, and reorder them. Likewise, if you get an assignment to *update* a document, first review, then improve organization if necessary. An astute audience can spot recycled documents—especially proposals—and audiences discount recycled documents.

6.3 Test Logic by Answering Five Questions.

After your draft passes the organization test, you can test for logic. Common sense is enough to find and fix most logical errors. However, some logical errors involve fact checking. Therefore, you need a subject matter expert—usually you—to find some of the logical errors. If you need to consult other subject matter experts, now is the time.

Experts in logic, from Aristotle onward, provide exhaustive works on logical errors or *fallacies*. These fallacies fall into two broad categories: about 40 nonlinguistic fallacies and five linguistic fallacies. Most nonlinguistic fallacies are true but irrelevant statements such as, *Everyone else is doing it*. Fortunately, we don't need to memorize all the fallacies to find and fix them. These five questions catch the nonlinguistic errors in logic:

1. What is the document's purpose?
2. So what?
3. Specified how?
4. Is it true?
5. Says who?

If the reader cannot find the *purpose of the document* in the first lines, the document has no premise. A premise is essential for logic. This problem is easy to fix with a good purpose statement, which you have if you did the analysis.

So what? catches most nonlinguistic logical fallacies. *Our solution is new . . ., we've always done it this way . . .*, all might be true but often irrelevant. This problem is easy to fix: Simply eliminate points and facts that fail the *So what* test. By completing analysis, you practically guarantee that your points are relevant and pass the *So what* test. You may still catch a few irrelevant facts.

Specified how? ensures you support your opinion or general truth with facts. Otherwise, you may have a generalization, another type of logical error. For example, *We didn't catch a fish today. Therefore, the lake has no more fish*—that is a sweeping generalization about the lake based on limited data. Or, you perhaps leap to a conclusion that does not follow the points: *I heard thunder, then it rained; therefore, thunder caused the rain.* You need to specify the intermediate steps in your logic. You fix this problem by gathering more information: *Clouds cause lightning; lightening causes thunder. Therefore, thunder indicates the presence of clouds that can cause rain.* You don't need to prove every point to an audience who does not need proof; therefore, ask *specified how* from the audience's point of view.

Is it true? deals with fact checking. An accidental error in fact is an error in logic. A deliberate error in fact is a lie—and also an error in logic. Ultimately, you need to know whether your facts are true. The definition of "The Big Lie," in George Orwell's famous book *1984,* is a statement that answers the *so what* question by offering relevant points, and seems to satisfy *specified how* by offering compelling facts, except that those facts are false. For example, in August 1835, the *New York Sun* published an article claiming that astronomist Sir John Hershel discovered a civilization on the moon. The article was full of facts, but all the facts were false. If you know your subject, this problem is easy to fix. Remove errors in fact, and select accurate facts.

Says who? prevents us from making false appeals to authority. For example, most celebrity endorsements are logical errors because the celebrity is not an expert on the product. Anonymous authorities are errors in logic: *Experts agree . . .* or *A news article claimed . . .* Being in print does not make something true. *Says who* often deals with policy and ethics. Sometimes you need to cite the policy, the law, or religion. Sometimes, *you* are the authority.

Let's use the five questions to test the following complaint letter's logic:

Dear Bank Customer Service:

We have been doing business with your bank for 10 years. [*The letter has no purpose statement, therefore, no premise.*] We have substantial demand deposit, money market, sweep, and payroll accounts at the McLean branch. [*So what? We take good care of our small accounts, too.*] We were shocked to see a charge on our statement that we did not authorize. [*So what? Shocked? See a therapist.*] Putting false charges on an invoice may be fraud. [*Says who? and So what?*] Enclosed is a copy of our recent VISA bill, March 8, Greenspan & Co., Inc. for $520.97. [*Finally, something relevant.*]

We believe we are victims of identity theft. [*Specify how? Any supporting facts?*] I queried our accounts payable department. [*So what?*] They have no idea where this bill came from. [*So what?*] We did not place an order with or receive anything from Greenspan & Co. [*Relevant to dispute.*] We have a purchase order system [*So what?*] and I would have known if I had approved any request involving the Greenspan. [*So what? Nobody is questioning your competence.*]

Without the logical fallacies the complaint letter reads:

This letter notifies you of a $520.97 unauthorized charge to my
account. Please remove the unauthorized charge.

Enclosed please find a copy of our recent VISA bill. The dis-
puted charge is March 8, made by Greenspan & Co., Inc. for
$520.97. We did not place an order with or receive anything
from Greenspan & Co.

Please call or write if you need more information.

Edit for Coherence

With your document's organization and logic confirmed, you can begin editing by adding coherence devices. These devices—both verbal and visual—make a document's logic more obvious to the reader. Coherence devices help the reader skim the document, follow the logical relationships within the document, or refer back to parts of the document.

Consider the interstate highway system with all its overpasses, entrance and exit ramps, bridges, and beltways around cities: an impressive feat of engineering. Now, imagine no highway signs. The logic of the highway system remains, but without the signs we can't take advantage of the logic. Coherence devices function like those highway signs, guiding the reader and making the document more useful. A document with zero coherence devices is just one huge block paragraph.

Coherence devices are useless on a document that lacks logic. An illogical document might as well be one huge block paragraph.

Already, your document has some important verbal devices. For example, in the introduction, the purpose statement and plan of the document state the overall logic and organization of the document.

Already, your document has some important visual devices. For example, the white space signifying paragraph breaks separates ideas.

Use six techniques to ensure that your documents have coherence:

7.1 Repeat key words throughout your document.
7.2 Ensure that each paragraph begins with a point.
7.3 Use transition words.
7.4 Use vertical lists for series of like items.

7.5 Ensure your graphics make a point.

7.6 Apply visual devices.

Edit for coherence before you edit for clarity or economy. If your readers can't follow your thoughts, they can't go further—even if you excel in your other editing techniques. Editing for coherence helps you discover any gaps in logic as you emphasize the order of your points and facts.

7.1 Repeat Key Words throughout Your Document.

The technique to repeat key words may seem odd at first. After all, when we were in grade school and we repeated words throughout the document, the teacher told us, *"Vary your word choice. . . . Use a thesaurus. . . . "* Many books about writing unwittingly encourage the same. The advice to vary our word choice is the worst advice we ever received about writing.

The correct advice is, *Never introduce a new word into your document without a good reason—and variety is not a good reason.* This advice applies when you write poetry, fiction, and especially nonfiction. Good reasons for introducing new words include making distinctions. Also, a poet may choose a word for rhyme, meter, or alliteration.

Why do teachers and writers give this bad advice? Our teachers were trying to get us to increase our vocabulary. However, we don't increase our vocabulary when we write; we increase our vocabulary when we read. Also, most teachers and professional writers enjoy some playfulness with words. I, too, enjoy word play that often involves shifting words. For example, in the classic TV comedy M★A★S★H, we hear this exchange:

Hawkeye: Radar, you look *pensive*.
Radar: No, I'm just *thinking*.
(*The Korean Doctor,* Season 5, Episode 9, 11/23/1976.)

Unless you are writing comedy, don't shift words.

Shifting words leads to a logical fallacy. Aristotle says by way of example, "if the point concerns a doublet, then draw the conclusion of a doublet, not of a *cloak.*" (*On Sophistical Refutations*)

Shifting words confuses the reader. When you tell an engineer about your *approach,* then *process, procedure,* and *method,* the engineer presumes you meant four different things. *Requirements* shift to *standards. Costs* shift to *investment. Facility* shifts to *building* to *factory* to *plant.* Do these words mean the same thing? Only the author knows for sure.

Repeat key words to make distinctions. For example, you conduct safety inspections. You need to make a distinction between *regulations* and *company policy.* Good, but if you add other words like *mandates, statutes, standards, procedures, obligations,* or *requirements,* your careful distinction between *regulation* and *policy* falls apart.

Repeat key words throughout the document. For example, use the key words in your purpose statement for your subject line of letters and memos.

Subheads need to be key words. Use the key words in the purpose statement or organization plan for your section subheads. For example: "This memo explains the *costs and benefits of leasing. . . .*" Your first section subhead is *Costs of Leasing,* and the second is *Benefits of Leasing.*

Because subheads are key words, the test that follows must quickly repeat the key words in the subhead. Otherwise, the subhead does not logically represent the text. For example, if the subhead is *Repeat key words throughout your document,* the reader needs to see the words *repeat, key words, throughout,* and *document* soon after reading the subhead. Standard subheads like *Introduction* and *Conclusion* are exempt.

Repeating key words helps the reader follow the point of the paragraph. For example, the following paragraph is hard to understand because of the many shifts:

The *computational tools* used to acquire specific wave impact *data* were *mounted* on the bow of the *ship*. The *measurements' accuracy* depends on the *installation* of the *instrumentation*, the hull design of the *vessel, ship speed,* and wave *height*. Increased *velocity* and wave *size* can cause *false readings* from the *sensors*.

The key word shifts above include the following:

computational tool = instrumentation = sensors
data = measurements = readings
mounted = installation
ship = vessel
speed = velocity
height = size
accuracy = false

When we repeat key words, the paragraph becomes coherent:

We installed sensors on the bow of the ship to measure wave impact. Measurement accuracy depends on the installation of the sensors, the ship's hull design, ship speed, and wave height. Increased ship speed and wave height can cause inaccurate measurements.

Repeat key words to tie graphics to your paragraph text. Repeat key words in headers and footers to help readers keep track of their place in the document.

Later when you edit, you can combine sentences or make a vertical list to avoid unnecessary repetition. However, right now you just need to make sure the words don't shift.

7.2 Ensure That Each Paragraph Begins with a Point.

Make a final check to ensure that each paragraph begins with a point—*and only one point*. If you followed your sentence outline when writing your draft, your paragraphs automatically begin with points. However, even veteran writers occasionally stray.

Avoid beginning paragraphs with a sentence that has more than one thought. These sentences make the reader guess which thought is the point of the paragraph. For example: *The chemical reaction was hard to predict* [thought one] *because the operator failed to follow the standard procedure* [thought two]. The reader must guess which of the two thoughts you intend to develop in the paragraph. Is the paragraph about your difficulty predicting the chemical reaction? Or is the paragraph about the operator not following procedure? Immediately, the paragraph lacks coherence.

Short sentences are best. Break the sentence mentioned in the previous example into simple sentences, and put the point of the paragraph first: *The chemical reaction was hard to predict.* The operator's failure becomes a supporting fact.

You can begin a paragraph with a more complex sentence if you need to transition from the previous paragraph. For example, you transition from a paragraph about a fixed-price contract to a paragraph about off-the-shelf technology:

Because the contract is fixed price, [the previous paragraph was about the fixed-price contract], we must use off-the-shelf technology [the current paragraph is about the need to use off-the-shelf technology].

If possible, a simple sentence is better:

We must use off-the-shelf technology to reduce the risks of our fixed-price contract.

Use short paragraphs to emphasize important points. You may occasionally use a one-sentence paragraph for emphasis, but the idea must stand by itself without supporting facts. Business letters often use a short initial paragraph to get to the point and grab attention. The letter continues with longer paragraphs to explain and expand points. Then the letter closes with a short paragraph calling for action—*what happens next.*

7.3 Use Transition Words.

Transition words tell the reader whether the next point or fact *progresses, recalls, reinforces,* or *contradicts* the previous point or facts. The following is just a partial list of transition words:

Progress	Recall	Reinforce	Contradict
Consequently	As mentioned	For example	Although
First, second	Because	For instance	Despite
Later	Before	Furthermore	However
Next	Earlier	In addition	In contrast
Subsequently	Formerly	In summary	Nevertheless
Then	Previously	Overall	On the other hand
Therefore	Remember	Specifically	Regardless

Transition words help the reader anticipate the relationship of the next point or fact. Therefore, put the transition at the beginning of the sentence or clause.

> Poor: Our plane landed one hour late in Frankfurt. We made, *however,* our connection to Lisbon.
>
> Good: Our plane landed one hour late in Frankfurt. *However,* we made our connection to Lisbon.

The transition word can also tell the reader if the points or facts are related by time or if one point or fact causes the other. Does A cause B, or does A merely relate in time to B? The distinction between cause and time is important for science and business.

Many writers confuse *since* with *because.* For example: *Since we installed the new software, our computer crashed.* Do you mean that the computer crashed *after* installing the software, or do you mean that the new software *caused* the crash? Use *because* if the software caused the crash.

Writers also confuse *while* with *although. While we installed the new software, our computer crashed*, means the computer crashed *during* the installation of the new software. If you mean that the system crashed *despite* the new software, then you need the word *although*.

Do not use *This means that . . .* or *It means . . .* to transition. We use these expressions as a crutch to transition when we speak. Replace these expressions with other transition words such as *therefore, consequently, specifically*, and so on.

In formal papers do not begin sentences with these three words: *and, or, but.* We often use these words to transition in conversation and in less formal documents. However, in formal documents, you use other transaction words: *in addition* or *furthermore* instead of *and*. You can use *although* or *however* instead of *but*.

7.4 Use Vertical Lists for Series of Like Items.

A vertical list is merely a series of like items. The like items can be whole sentences or small details. Because the items are alike, they are *all* whole sentences or they are *all* small details. If the sentences or details relate in any way more complicated than a series, write a paragraph, not a vertical list. The most common problem in a vertical list is that the items are not alike.

Follow two rules to make your vertical lists work:

1. Introduce each list by defining the series.
2. Make the list items grammatically parallel (alike).

Define the series by naming the like items and stating how they are logically related. In addition, tell the reader how many items you have in the list. We recommend you number your list items. Bullets have better eye appeal, but numbers are better for reference. Avoid using letters—a, b, c—because the reader must translate numbers to letters. Numbers do not necessarily imply order or ranking: The definition of the series does.

Using numbers for list items improves coherence three ways. First, if your list continues through a page break, your reader knows to turn the page to finish the list. If you have a long list, numbers help you refer back to items—you can more easily refer to *list item twelve* rather than *the third bullet from the bottom of the page*. If you have a list followed immediately by another list, numbers put clean boundaries on the lists, whereas bullets tend to run together.

Make your list's items grammatically parallel. Parallelism refers to using the same grammar for logically similar sentences and parts of sentences. Therefore, all the list items are complete sentences, or all list items are not. If one sentence is a question, all sentences must be questions. If one list item begins with a verb, they all begin with a verb and so on. If you have a difficult time making a list item parallel, consider the strong possibility that the list item is not part of the series.

The most important benefit from using the two rules of making lists is that you catch errors in logic. For example, I paraphrase below a list from a vintage 1968 Volkswagen repair manual I used when replacing worn-out valves.

> With the engine safely removed from the car, follow these three steps to extract the valves:

1. Remove the four valve stems by hand, exposing each by rotating the drive shaft.
2. Tap out the old valve sleeves. You will need Volkswagen special tool VW. Ser 1359-63, available at most dealers.
3. Although the valve stems may be reusable, we recommend you install new valve stems and valve sleeves.

What's wrong with this list? The definition of the series is good and the numbers are helpful, but the list items have two logical errors. The second list item has commentary about the *special tool*. Try to keep commentary out of your verticals lists. In this case, the commentary is too late. I wish I had known to go to the VW dealer to buy the special tool while I still had an engine in my car. List item three is not a step. Another clue is that list item three is not grammatically parallel. Items one and two are commands and item three is a recommendation. The revised list follows:

> Before you begin, ensure you have Volkswagen special tool VW. Ser 1359-63, available at most authorized dealers. [In the introduction before you remove the engine.]

With the engine safely removed from the car, follow two steps
to extract the valves:

1. Remove the four valve stems by hand, exposing each by
   rotating the drive shaft.
2. Tap out the old valve sleeves using the special tool.

Although the valve stems may be reusable, we recommend you
install new valve stems and valve sleeves.

Avoid imbedding a vertical list within a vertical list. Imbedded lists
read like computer program code. Consider using a table instead.
For example, a laboratory report may show a table to summarize
series of data about the experiment.

The toxicity experiment involved four study groups sorted by
sex, dose level, and dose concentration:

	No. of Mice		Dose Level	Dose Concentration
Group	Male	Female	(mg/kg/day)	(mg/mL)
1 (Control)	10	10	0	0
2 (Low)	10	10	100	10
3 (Mid)	10	10	300	30
4 (High)	10	10	1,000	100

Avoid long lists, especially when writing instructions. *Follow these
57 steps to assemble the tricycle* is daunting. If necessary, break long
complicated tasks into subtasks: *Follow these four steps to assemble the
handlebars. . . . Follow these five steps to assemble and adjust the seat. . . .*

Avoid long list items. If you have more than two sentences in a list item, you probably have commentary or a paragraph. Pull commentary out of your list items and write the commentary as paragraphs.

List punctuation varies depending on the style guide. Choose a style guide and be consistent.

7.5 Ensure Your Graphics Make a Point.

For any kind of graphic—including tables, figures, graphs, and pictures—follow this simple four-part logic to make your point:

1. Introduce the graphic by telling readers what they *learn*—the point.
2. Show relationships in the data that make the point.
3. Label parts of the graphic as needed.
4. Comment about the graphic to support the point.

If you cannot tell the readers what they learn from your graphic, it is at best *eye wash,* or worse, *misleading.* Some experts argue that they do not need to tell readers what to learn from the graphic because their data are compelling. Really? The data might compel the author, but smart people draw the wrong conclusions from the right data every day.

Captions for pictures need to tell readers what they learn from the picture. For example, naval architects prepare a document on boat design and safety in which they include a picture of crash tests featuring crash dummies. The caption reads: *Note the location of the crash dummy's head.* What? Is this one of those hidden picture puzzles for children? The caption needs to tell the picture's teaching point: *Tests show that standard cockpit designs contribute to head injuries in low-speed collisions.*

To show relationships within the data, you must first strip out variables that do not relate to your point. Unfortunately, many experts share *all* their data. They researched 27 variables, and by golly, they are going to give the reader data on all 27, even though only two variables correlate. You can archive your data in an appendix for future analysis, but inside your document, limit your graphics and tables to the relevant variables.

Label parts of your graphics as needed. A veterinarian pharmaceutical company publishes a document about chicken vaccines. The document has a picture of a chicken's foot and the good caption: *Vaccinated chickens developed foot lesions as shown in the picture.* To help readers who can't tell the difference between a healthy bump on the chicken foot and a lesion, draw a thin line to the lesion and add a label. Also, make sure your labels use the same key words in your text.

Comment about the graphic *after* you show it. Make sure you repeat the key terms used to introduce and label the graphic. With the point and the graphic fresh in the readers' minds, they can better understand your comments. This order is key, and merits repeating: introduce, show, then comment.

Keep the graphic with the text. Layout artists sometimes make the mistake of moving the graphic away from the text, sacrificing the logic for a prettier design. Long ago, printers put all the graphics in an appendix because they lacked the technology to integrate the graphics with the text. Now, technology makes integrating graphics with text easy—much better for readers.

The following case demonstrates the importance of graphics used to make a clear point. On January 27, 1986, the day before a space shuttle launch, Morton Thiokol reacted to the weather forecast—temperatures falling to 26 degrees at Cape Canaveral. Morton Thiokol engineers worried that at freezing temperatures the rubber

O-Rings on their solid fuel rockets might fail to keep the hot gases from leaking and causing damage. They recommended against the launch and NASA balked, saying they were "appalled" at the recommendation. So Morton Thiokol retreated from their recommendation to rely on their data; they faxed NASA 13 charts filled with data about O-Ring performance. Some charts had data about O-Ring erosion, depth, and soot. Some charts showed evidence of *blow-by*—soot passing the O-Ring. Other charts had data about temperature and wind speed.

However, the charts did not clearly tell NASA what the data meant. After intense discussions about data—*not the points*—NASA drew the wrong conclusion: O-Rings survive in a wide range of weather conditions. The next morning, NASA launched despite freezing temperatures. The O-Rings failed. Seventy-three seconds in flight, the space shuttle exploded, killing the seven astronauts.

Morton Thiokol did not follow these four principles of using tables, figures, graphs, and pictures. Let's see how these four principles can help.

First, tell NASA what to learn from the graphics: *O-Ring damage increases as temperature decreases.* (Note: If your client rejects your recommendation, do not retreat to the data. Your fallback position is the general truth.) Leading with this simple point might be enough to save the shuttle. With this point, NASA can better evaluate the data. They know that the only two variables in discussion are O-Ring damage and temperature. They are more likely to see the causal relationship in the data. The other variables such as blow-by, soot, and wind speed are not key to the decision.

Second, show relationships in the data. The chart in Figure 7.1 shows the O-Ring damage in relation to temperature for the previous 24 launches. Irrelevant variables are gone and no longer distract.

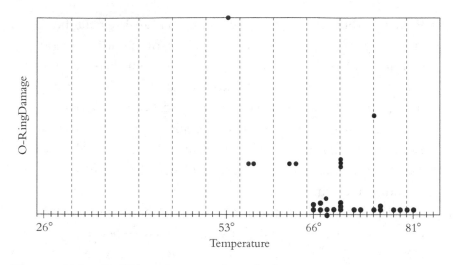

Figure 7.1   O-Ring damage in relation to temperature

Third, label the graphic. The chart in Figure 7.2 adds information by labeling the trend with a line and focusing attention to the temperature level—66 degrees—where O-Ring damage is likely.

Fourth, provide comments: The O-Rings are a failsafe device. Therefore, proper function is to have zero O-Ring damage. Most launches above 66 degrees had zero or negligible O-Ring damage. All launches below 66 degrees had O-Ring damage. At the 53-degree launch, O-Ring damage was particularly severe. More than a third of the circumference of the primary O-Ring was destroyed. The secondary O-Ring had damage but survived.

In this example, you see that data is not, by itself, compelling. You need to make your point as an opinion or general truth. Remember that if your opinion causes a protest, fall back to the general truth—not the data. This example also shows the power of graphics to transform data into useful information in support of a point. (For a more thorough treatment of graphics, see Edward Tufte's *Visual Explanations* [Cheshire, CT: Graphics Press, 1997])

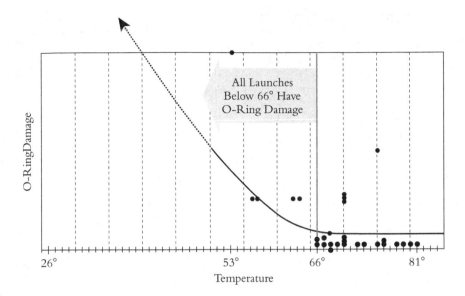

Figure 7.2 O-Ring damage in relation to temperature

The most important part of this logic is to tell the readers what they learn from the graphic. You may have zero talent as a graphic artist, but you can control this part of the logic. Also, if you can explain to a graphic artist what readers are supposed to learn, the artist can design a better graphic. Instead of telling the artist, "We need a graphic that shows all the O-Ring data we've collected," tell the artist, "We need a graphic that teaches NASA that O-Ring damage correlates with temperature."

7.6 Apply Visual Devices.

In the age of the mechanical typewriter, the author had few options for applying visual devices. Layout designers, publishers, and type-setters made those decisions. Now, the personal computer and

Typography is ink on the page:	_Layout is placement of ink on the page:_
• Different TYPEFACES	• Page orientation
• _Italics_, **bold,** <u>underline</u>	• Margins
• List bullets, numbers, letters	• Footers and headers
• Ruling lines, boxes, screens	• Indent, outdent, center, justification
• Icons	• Line spacing
• Graphics	• White space
• Color	• Rows and columns

word processing software shift many of those decisions about visual devices to you, the author.

Visual devices fall into two categories: typography and layout.

Use visual devices with a sense of purpose. Don't add visual devices just because your software allows it. Help your readers _skim read_ by visually highlighting key words, headings, and sentences. Help your readers _follow the logic_ by using different fonts, white space, indentations, ruling lines, boxes, columns, and vertical lists to group and order the information. Help your readers _refer_ back to your document with footers and headers, numbers, letters, and tabs.

Do not go overboard with fonts. A font is defined by typeface and point size. Your word processor probably has more than one hundred fonts. Limit your typeface to one serif (like Times Roman) and one sans serif (like Arial). With each typeface, you can make Normal, **Bold**, _Italics_, and <u>Underline</u>. Rarely do you need **_Bold Italics_**. Limit yourself to five point sizes. Use bold to draw attention. Use italics rather than quote marks to show words used in a special way. Reserve quote marks for quotations.

Over _use_ of fonts makes **_your_** text **look** like a ransom note **cut-and-pasted** from **newspapers**.

Edit for Clarity

Clarity is the most important style edit. Your goal for the clarity edit is that each sentence has only one interpretation. If your document tells your readers what they need to know, in the right order, and has only one interpretation, your document succeeds.

Use these seven techniques to ensure that your sentences are clear:

8.1 Use concrete and specific words.

8.2 Use active voice.

8.3 Simplify tense: Stay in present tense when possible.

8.4 Avoid the helping verbs *would*, *should*, and *could*.

8.5 Identify and replace ambiguous pronouns.

8.6 Use standard English words.

8.7 Check sentences for misplaced or dangling modifiers.

Much ambiguity comes from bad habits we learned in school. In our effort to avoid repeating words and the pronoun *I*, we used passive voice. Our teachers encouraged us to demonstrate our mastery of all 12 verb tenses, whether useful or not. They suggested we use helping verbs such as *would, should,* and *could* to create a *nicer* tone. All these bad habits cause ambiguity.

Some scientists defend ambiguous language because they cannot be certain if their theories work or their experiments are accurate. They fear false precision. Lawyers sometimes defend ambiguous language in contracts because they cannot foresee every contingency. They do not want to create unnecessary restrictions or create loopholes by omitting a contingency. Although these problems are real, ambiguous language is the wrong remedy.

Imprecise data or unforeseen contingencies are *limitations*. Rather than use ambiguous language in the body, acknowledge the limitations in your introduction, then do your best to overcome the limitations when you write clearly in the body of your document.

Ambiguous language is the *worst* way to write about uncertain subject matter—the *worst* way to address unforeseen contingencies. Ambiguity causes technical, economic, legal, and ethical risks. Ambiguity perpetuates errors. In a healthy organization, authors prefer to be clearly wrong than ambiguous. Then, a colleague can catch the mistake. Unfortunately, too many managers punish clear communication, then wonder why they can't get a straight answer.

Moreover, ambiguous language is unnecessary. You can write clearly about uncertain subjects. *The test was inconclusive* is a perfectly clear sentence. You can clearly qualify statements: *Using current labor and material rates, we estimate the cost of the project to be between $1.8 million and $1.95 million.* You can clearly allow for unforeseen contingencies: *The change management committee shall review additional requirements, designs, and costs before issuing a task order.*

Anybody who purposefully makes a clear text ambiguous is no friend of the truth.

From Aristotle onward, philosophers cite ambiguity as a logical fallacy. Some ambiguity infects our documents because English words often have multiple meanings. English sentence structure can also cause multiple meanings. Sometimes ambiguity is unintentional. Nevertheless, these logical fallacies are real, and they cause real risks. We need to do our best to remove as much ambiguity as possible.

Most authors check for clarity by rereading their document to make sure they understand the sentences. *Of course you understand your own sentences; you wrote them.* The problem is not you or your logic. Your analysis, sentence outline, draft, revision, and edit for coherence are all good.

The problem is the English language and your incredible brain. English has inherent ambiguities: vague words, passive voice, future tense, subjunctive mood, ambiguous pronouns, and modifiers. When you read your own text, you automatically compensate for what is lacking in the text's clarity. Without giving the matter any thought, you see the specific meaning behind the vague word. You know the hidden actor behind the passive voice. You know if the verb tense matters. You know the specific condition implied vaguely in the *would*, *should*, or *could*. You know what the ambiguous pronoun refers to. Your poor reader doesn't have your insights and thereby gets lost in text that seems clear to you.

For these same reasons, you are the only person who can confidently edit your text for clarity. Editors cannot read your mind. A good editor can find the ambiguity in your text, but you need to fix it.

Attack ambiguity at the word level with *pattern recognition*. You make a quick pass through the document—less than a minute per page—marking ambiguous text. If you find yourself taking more than a minute per page to mark text, you are reading and not using pattern recognition. After you mark all the ambiguous text, you go back and fix the problems.

Stick with our system of marking and fixing ambiguous text. You get a surprising benefit. These repetitive mechanical steps become part of your language instinct. Slowly but surely, you stop using passive voice, unnecessary tenses, ambiguous pronouns, and other causes of ambiguity.

8.1 Use Concrete and Specific Words.

Replace abstract and general words with concrete and specific words. Abstract and general words allow multiple interpretations. Concrete words engage the five senses: see, hear, touch, smell, and taste. Specific words include real names, times, places, and numbers. Consequently, concrete and specific words are more precise and, therefore, interesting. Abstract and general words are ambiguous and, therefore, dull:

> The food (*general*) was appealing (*abstract*).
> The warm bread with nut-brown crust and yeasty aroma made my mouth water (*concrete and specific*).

Your authority as a writer comes from your concrete and specific words, not your education or job title. If your facts are abstract and general, your reader can assume either you don't know the concrete and specific facts, or you do know, but you are unwilling to share those facts with the reader. In either case, the reader has reason to distrust you.

Ironically, if your subject matter seems abstract, you need to make a greater effort to use concrete and specific words. For example, computer science can be abstract; therefore, we use concrete words such as *click, drag, drop, point with a mouse*—not *actuate by means of an input device.*

Make your modifiers specific and concrete. Modifiers like *several, numerous,* and *various* don't add value. If you write *several options,* the word *options* is already plural and the word *several* means plural. Eliminate *several* or substitute a number: *We have at least four options.* Avoid vague modifiers like *very, extremely, dramatic, vital.* . . . Mark Twain sarcastically suggests that whenever you use the word *very,* you might as well substitute the word *damn.* Either eliminate the vague modifier, or substitute concrete and specific words. Instead of writing *An overdose of Tylenol™ can be very dangerous,* write *An overdose of Tylenol™ can cause liver damage.*

Being concrete and specific may require more words. For example, *Remove the old finish* is short, but vague. *Scrape or sand off the four layers of old paint* is longer, but clear. Remember, clarity is our chief style concern.

Compare the following pair of sentences, and notice how concrete and specific words are clearer and have more authority:

> A number of factors (*how many? what's a factor?*) must be addressed (*how? by whom?*) to ensure (*how?*) this effort (*what effort?*) meets its objectives (*how?*) within the proposed time frame (*when?*).
>
> Our IT Manager must test the wireless router for data security before Software, Inc. can launch our Intranet next month.

8.2 Use Active Voice.

In English, a verb can be in active or passive voice. Use active voice for clarity. In active voice, the subject of the sentence performs the action: *Fred updates the system.* The subject *Fred* acts. Every active voice sentence follows the clear pattern:

- *Who does what*—Bob hit the ball.
- *What does what*—The ball flew over the fence.

In passive voice, the subject of the sentence does not perform the action: *The system was updated.* The subject *system* does not act— or does it? Maybe the system updated itself. Because of passive voice, we don't know; therefore, we must guess.

The problem with passive voice is that the reader must guess *who* or *what* performs the action. Readers guess wrong about half the time, and those wrong guesses waste time and cause unnecessary risk.

Passive voice is appropriate for three reasons: when the actor is unknown, unimportant, or embarrassed.

1. Unknown—My umbrella was stolen.
2. Unimportant—The control group was given a placebo.
3. Embarrassed—You were improperly invoiced $200 instead of $20.

In academic writing, many actors remain unknown. Because many secondary sources report facts in passive voice, we can't know who or what did the action. We can research further—usually in vain—to determine the actor, or we can pass along the passive voice: a garbage-in, garbage-out situation.

Some documents tolerate passive voice better than others. In scientific papers, the protocol of an experiment often has passive voice: *The rats were injected.* We don't care who injected the rats, and if we guess wrong, nothing bad happens. However, even in protocols, we can write in active voice: *Each rat received an injection.*

On the other hand, passive voice in contracts or instructions is intolerable. We need the accountability. We need to know *who does what* and *what does what.* Passive voice causes expensive misunderstandings in proposals, contracts, design documents, procedures, policies, and instruction manuals.

The first step in eliminating passive voice is finding and marking it. Using pattern recognition—*not by reading*—look through your text until you see some form of the verb *to be: be, being, am, is, are, was, were, been.* Stop. Now look to the right for another verb. If you see another verb, ask yourself: Does the reader know *who* or *what* performs the action in the second verb? If the sentence meets all three conditions—*to be* verb, plus second verb, and does not answer *who* or *what*—the sentence is passive. For example: The ball *was* [a *to be* verb] *hit* [another verb]. Do we know *who* or *what* hit the ball? No. The sentence is passive.

After you mark the passive voice, answer the question *who does what* or *what does what* to change the sentence to active voice.

This edit is easy. For example: *The shoreline was destroyed.* *Who or what* destroyed the shoreline? You know the answer: a tsunami. Make the answer the subject of the revised sentence: *A tsunami destroyed the shoreline.*

The tickets were purchased. (*who* purchased?)
Dave purchased the tickets.
The report is automatically printed. (*what* prints?)
One-Rite software automatically prints the report.

Avoid answering the question by adding the *by whom* or *by what* at the end of the passive voice. *The tickets were purchased by Dave* is still passive, although an improvement. The phrase *by Dave* is a modifier and modifiers can cause sentence structure problems. For example: *The tickets were purchased for the opera by Dave.* Oops—*by Dave* is misplaced. He purchased the tickets, but the sentence says that he wrote the opera.

Academic and scientific writing often suffer from passive voice. They don't want to use the pronoun *I* or *we* in formal documents. Instead of writing *I determined that the drug is safe,* they write *The drug was determined to be safe,* or even worse, *It was determined that the drug is safe.* The best way to change the sentence to active voice is to let your work speak for you: *The study indicates, the pattern shows, the data suggest, the correlation implies, the experiment provides. . . .* The result is a "what does what" sentence. Note how the following academic sentence improves when we change it to a "what does what," active voice sentence:

The pipe weld *was given* a careful examination, and it *was deter-mined* that a filler substance in the weld caused the leak.

A careful examination of the pipe weld showed that a filler sub-stance in the weld caused the leak.

You can also cut passive voice by eliminating actions that the reader does not need to know. Indeed, about half of all pas-sive voice is about actions that the reader doesn't need to know. For example: *The ferry is designed to transport 120 automobiles.* If the *design* is not an action the reader needs to know, eliminate the whole action: *The ferry transports 120 automobiles.* If the design is an issue, then tell the reader *who* or *what* designed the ferry: *Hyundai designed the ferry to transport 120 automobiles.* In most cases, the reader doesn't need to know about the actions *is designed, is considered, is expected,* or *is intended.*

Here are two more edits of passive voice where we simply elim-inated the action:

The copier *is located* on the third floor. (Reader doesn't care who *located* the copier.)

The copier is on the third floor.

The new price was calculated to return 7 percent on costs of goods sold. (Reader doesn't care who *calculated* the return.)

The new price returns 7 percent on costs of goods sold.

Whenever the passive voice follows a *who, which,* or *that,* you can usually cut the *who, which, that* plus the *to be* verb, thereby eliminat-ing the passive voice:

Mr. Smith, who *was* recently *promoted* to partner, gets a company car. (Reader doesn't care who *promoted* Mr. Smith.)

Mr. Smith, recently promoted to partner, gets a company car.

The study group *was comprised* of 50 males that *were selected* at random. (Reader doesn't care who *comprised* or *selected* the study group.)

The study group was 50 males selected at random.

Often you can choose which technique to use to eliminate the passive voice. As the author, you are the best qualified to make the choice. The result is always a *who does what* or *what does what* sentence.

Passive: The paint *is* then *allowed* to dry for one hour.

What does what: The paint dries one hour.

Who does what: Allow the paint to dry one hour.

Passive: The investigation *is started* only after a legal complaint *has been submitted*.

What does what: The investigation starts only after a legal complaint.

Who does what: The police start an investigation only after a citizen submits a legal complaint.

Remember, you are the only person who can confidently fix the ambiguity of passive voice. You know *who* or *what* does the action. You know whether the reader needs to know *who* or *what* did the action.

8.3 Simplify Tense: Stay in Present Tense When Possible.

Tense is the form of the verb that tells the reader *when* the action happens. In technical documents, most actions happen in the present or the past.

English has twelve tenses:

1. Present	I write.
2. Past	I wrote.
3. Future	I will write.
4. Present perfect	I have written.
5. Past perfect	I had written.
6. Future perfect	I will have written.
7. Present progressive	I am writing.
8. Past progressive	I was writing.
9. Future progressive	I will be writing.
10. Present perfect progressive	I have been writing.
11. Past perfect progressive	I had been writing.
12. Future perfect progressive	I will have been writing.

Some languages have more than twelve tenses, some less. In fact, all languages have only one tense in common—present tense, because present tense is the only reality. All other tenses are a function of our imagination. Because the *real* is always clearer than imagination, use the present tense as much as possible. Write your draft as you speak, then edit by simplifying past, future, perfect, and progressive tense verbs.

The past tense is useful and natural in English, but sometimes misleads. All of us experienced living in the past, but we remember things differently. If you want to test that theory, just go to a family reunion. For example, *Joan claimed that she caught a cold* is in past tense and has room for misinterpretation. Has Joan recanted her claim? Do we infer that she is better now? *Joan claims she has a cold* is present tense and has no room for misinterpretation.

The future tense is a serious problem. No one lives or has knowledge of the future. Therefore, any statement about the future is speculative and more likely to be ambiguous. Moreover, speculative statements lack conviction. Mark every pattern where you see the word *will* used in front of another verb. The fix is easy. Either *will* falls out painlessly or you leave it in.

Engineers have the habit of writing in future tense. After all, they usually write about things they propose to build, maintain, or operate in the future. Naturally, they write their drafts in future tense. Unfortunately, future tense is speculative, lacking conviction. Future tense is less persuasive.

Compare two sentences in a technical proposal:

The new perpetual inventory system *will save* 2,000 labor hours each year.

The new perpetual inventory system *saves* 2,000 labor hours each year.

The smoke detector *will* operate up to one year on a C battery.

The smoke detector operates up to one year on a C battery.

Which sentences show your conviction? The present tense, of course. Write proposals, contracts, designs, and manuals with conviction—use present tense.

However, let's say that your statement about *saving 2,000 labor hours* really is speculative—is the word *will* appropriate then? No. The word *will* is still a problem for another, and seemingly contradictory, reason. The word *will* used as a condition means that the action is mandatory, a command. If I tell my children, *You will clean your bedrooms,* they know from my tone of voice that I am not speculating about the future. I just issued a command. Documents cannot convey that same tone of voice.

Therefore, if you need to imply that *saving 2,000 labor hours* is speculative, use another word to show that speculative condition: *may, might,* or *can save 2,000 labor hours.* Lawyers avoid the word *will* in contracts to avoid confusing tense and command. Instead, they use the words *must* or *shall* to show the action is mandatory. For example, *The tenant will pay for the damage.* Do you mean the payment is in the future, or do you mean the payment is mandatory? *The tenant shall pay for the damage* has only one interpretation and is clear.

The perfect tense refers to an action completed (perfected) in the present, past, or future. The perfect tense is a nuisance problem, usually implying subtle distinctions that don't exist. The perfect tense rarely makes a useful distinction. What is the useful distinction between these three sentences?

> We have received your application. (present perfect)
> We received your application. (past)
> We have your application. (present)

Mark every pattern where you see a *has, have,* or *had* in front of another verb. The fix is easy. Either the *has, have,* or *had* falls out painlessly, or you leave it in. The perfect tense falls out painlessly more than 90 percent of the time. Occasionally, you need the subtle distinction of a perfect tense. For example: *For more than 300 years, The College of William and Mary has provided excellent liberal arts education.* If you cut the *has,* your statement suggests that the college stopped providing excellent education. Trust your instinct as you edit the perfect tense.

The progressive tense refers to an ongoing action. The pattern for the progressive tense is a "to be" verb in front of a verb ending in *−ing*: *The payroll system is running on an IBM computer.*

Sometimes, the progressive tense is useful and conveys exactly what you mean. *We are working on a solution to your problem* tells the reader that you intend to work until you get a solution—exactly what you want to say.

However, the progressive tense often exaggerates. Exaggerations cause ambiguity. For example, if the payroll system does not run continuously on the IBM computer, the progressive tense is an exaggeration. Drop the progressive tense and write in simple present tense, *The payroll system runs on an IBM computer.*

When you end a letter with the common phrase, *I am looking forward to seeing you*, the looking does not stop. From the moment you write *I am looking,* you can't eat, can't sleep, and so forth. The progressive tense exaggerates what you really mean: *I look forward to seeing you.*

Again, the fix is easy. Either the progressive tense falls out painlessly or you leave it in. Again, trust your instinct.

You get four additional benefits from simplifying tenses:

1. You shorten your sentences, making your sentences easier to read.
2. You add significance and precision to your remaining tenses when you remove tenses that serve no real purpose.
3. You eliminate the grammar error of shifting tenses within a series.
4. You help non-native English readers, who expect that the writer shifts tenses for a purpose.

For example, a purchasing agent in Spain reads, "ACME *will be invoicing* monthly." The Spanish-speaking agent, who knows grammar well, wonders why the writer uses the future progressive. Does the invoicing depend on future events? Does the invoicing ever stop? We can avoid this awkward confusion by simplifying the tense: "ACME *invoices* monthly."

8.4 Avoid the Helping Verbs *Would, Should,* and *Could.*

The verbs *would, should,* and *could* used in front of another verb vaguely imply a condition. Unfortunately, the reader cannot know what the condition is. Consider the range of possibilities. *Should* can mean:

May: Permissible	You may go.
Might: Possible	You might go.
Can: Possible	You can go.
Needs to: Possible and desired	You need to go.
Must or *shall:* Mandatory	You must go.

The range of meaning—from permissible to mandatory—causes the reader to guess. *Would, should,* and *could* are ambiguous.

Should is especially confusing. Most people think the first definition of *should* is in the *permissible-to-possible* range. When they read, "You *should* wear a helmet in the construction site," they hear a suggestion. However, all dictionaries say the first definition of *should* is *shall*, meaning mandatory. You can avoid this confusion by avoiding the word *should*. Write, "You must wear a helmet in the construction site."

If you do not want to imply a condition, just eliminate the *would, should,* or *could*. For example, the sign *You should not feed the bears,* allows for a condition in which you may feed the bears—what if the bears are starving? With the *should* removed, the sign has less room for misinterpretation: *Do not feed the bears*—no condition, just simple instruction.

If you need to imply a condition, use more specific and concrete language like *may, might, can, needs to, recommend, request, suggest, intend, prefer, must,* or *shall*. As you consider the following examples, notice which sentences have less room for misinterpretation:

You *should* wear your seatbelt low across your lap.

We recommend you wear your seatbelt low across your lap.

A thermoelectric cooler *would* satisfy the requirements.

A thermoelectric cooler satisfies the requirements.

Should you work more than 40 hours, you *would* take the next day off.

If you work more than 40 hours, you must take the next day off.

The customer *could* qualify to receive a refund.

The customer might qualify to receive a refund.

8.5 Identify and Replace Ambiguous Pronouns.

A pronoun is a word that stands in the place of a noun: person, place, thing, or action. The pronoun is ambiguous if it does not refer back to the closest person, place, thing, or action. The pronouns that cause the most trouble are *it, this, that, these,* and *those.*

Mark every *it* you see on the page. On average, half are fine; half are ambiguous. For each *it,* look backward in the text. If the *it* does not equal the first person, place, thing, or action, replace the *it* with a noun. Consider the following examples:

Jerry Coleman sports announcer: "There's a high fly ball! Winfield goes back, back . . . his head hits the wall . . . it's rolling towards second base." (Winfield just lost his head or the stadium lost a wall.)

We increased the dose of the drug. It proved ineffective. (What proved ineffective: the drug or the dose increase?)

Mark every *this, that, these,* and *those* used as pronouns. These words are perfectly good modifiers, telling the reader which item—*this* item—but the pronouns are ambiguous. For *this, that, these,* and *those,* ask, This *what?* That *what?* These *what?* Those *what?* Insert your answer after the pronoun. Replace phrases like *that's that, this means,* or *this means that* with a transition word such as *therefore:*

> Read this. (*This* what?)
> Read this warning label.
> We need to reconsider that. (*That* what?)
> We need to reconsider that cost.
> This means we must store old files in the attic. (*This means* is a
> transition.)
> Therefore, we must store old files in the attic.

Mark every sentence or clause that begins with *there* or *it* followed by a "to be" verb. We use the *it is* and *there are* beginnings as a crutch when we write our drafts. Unfortunately, the pronoun *there* is abstract. The verb *to be* merely indicates that something exists. So, *there are* just tells the reader that something abstract exists.

Fixing the *there are* and *it is* ambiguity is more complicated than fixing *this* or *it* pronouns. Often, you need to restructure the sentence. Use the w*ho does what, what does what* logic.

> It is necessary to use a purchase order for office supplies (*who
> does what?*).
> You need a purchase order for office supplies.
> There are ten key milestones in our management plan (*what does
> what?*).
> Our management plan has ten key milestones.

In formal academic and scientific writing, the *It is* opening combined with passive voice becomes a crutch to avoid using the pronouns *I* or *we*. Unfortunately, this bad habit can undermine the author's credibility. *It is widely accepted, known, understood,* or *believed* are logical fallacies. These statements appeal to an anonymous authority. *Widely known by whom?* Instead use phrases like *The medical community knows,* or *The pharmaceutical industry knows,* or *The American public knows,* or *I know. . . .*

It is and *there are* beginnings are abstract and boring. Notice how eliminating abstract beginnings makes your prose more lively. Compare the two versions of a tourist brochure:

> *There is* a sense of history in Easton, Maryland. *There are* streets lined with Victorian homes. Each Saturday during the spring, *there will be* garden tours hosted by the Easton Garden Society. (32 words)
>
> Easton, Maryland has a sense of history. Victorian homes line the streets. Each Saturday during the spring, the Easton Garden Society hosts garden tours. (24 words)

When you fix the *it is* and *there are* beginnings, you either add value, shorten the sentence, or both. However, don't obsess. Either fix the problem quickly or move on. Some sentences need the crutch. For example, *It is raining* is a natural expression, and alternatives may sound awkward.

Replacing ambiguous pronouns causes repetition. Don't worry about repetition now. Later, when you edit for economy, you can combine sentences or use vertical lists to cut the repetition.

Finally, other pronouns such as *he, his, she, hers, they, theirs,* and *which* also deserve a look:

> When Bob told his father *he* wrecked *his* car, *he* was upset. (Who wrecked the car? Who was upset?)
>
> Bob wrecked his car. He was upset when he told his father.

8.6 Use Standard English Words.

English already has enough words, about 1.2 million. We rarely need to supplement standard English words by using other languages or inventing words.

A hundred years ago, college students studied Latin and maybe some Greek. This educated class often used bits of Latin in conversation, almost as code to signify their level of education. If their families had money, they took the "Grand Tour" through France and Italy. These wealthy people used bits of French in conversation to signify their social status. Now, many people go to college, and many people can afford to fly to France. Using Latin and French was pompous a hundred years ago and is just plain silly today.

Don't use Latin words unless necessary. Latin is still necessary for legal and medical texts and bibliographic citations.

Even the most common bits of Latin confuse. Ask a roomful of professionals what *i.e.* means, and you get as many as five answers. The abbreviation *i.e.* stands for the Latin *id est*, or English *that is*.

Instead of using *i.e.* and *e.g.,* use English words like *meaning, defined as, such as, including, for example.* Avoid the Latin *via.* Instead, use more precise English words like *by way of, by means of, through,* or *using.* The Latin *etc.* might as well be translated as *I'm too lazy to finish this list.*

As a rule, don't invent words. If you invent words, you sound like the professional athlete who becomes a parody of erudition: *We must redoublify our efforts to encapturate our former intensification.* Translation: *We must practice harder.* Engineers are just as guilty when using phrases like, *We functionalized the process taskwise.* Translation: *We defined each process function by task.*

Use standard English words currently understood by most business and technical professionals. You can use recognized technical jargon for the reader who knows much about the information; otherwise, avoid jargon or define it. If you use jargon, choose concrete and specific words. For example, *system crash* is general jargon. Use more specific jargon such as, *The operating system software failed after a run-time error.*

Don't create compound words with a slash (/). Slashes are appropriate to show division, such as miles/hour. We also use slashes as separators in web addresses and dates. Unfortunately, many authors use the slash as shorthand to indicate a joining *and* or separating *or*. The space saved by the slash is insignificant and the ambiguity is substantial:

Send a copy of your *receipt/invoice* for a *credit/refund.*

The problem is that the reader does not know if a slash means *and* or *or*. Do I send the receipt *and* the invoice or do I have a choice? Do I get a credit *and* a refund, or just one? To eliminate the ambiguity, remove the slashes and substitute either *and* or *or*.

Send a copy of your *receipt and invoice* for a *credit or refund.*

A few words compounded with the slash have become standard English, such as *HIV/AIDS* in medicine and *client/server* in computer science.

The *and/or* causes confusion. The Kentucky Supreme Court says the *and/or* is a "much-condemned conjunctive-disjunctive crutch of sloppy thinkers." Ouch.

In almost every case, a simple *and* or a simple *or* suffices, but too many authors toss in the *and/or* to allow for theoretical possibilities. For example:

You can call *and/or* write to request a free estimate.

In theory, a person might call and write, but in practice a person either calls or writes. Stay practical; remove the *and/*:

You can call *or* write to request a free estimate.

Here is another example:

Our global portfolio invests in U.S. *and/or* foreign markets.

In theory, your global portfolio might invest exclusively in foreign markets, but in practice, you plan to invest some portion of the portfolio in U.S. markets. Stay practical; remove the */or:*

Our global portfolio invests in U.S. *and* foreign markets.

The worst *and/or* offenses occur when you have three or more items in the series:

The applicant must have at least five year's experience in finance, banking, sales, risk management, information systems, *and/or* human resource development.

With a series of six items, we calculate six factorial or 720 possible combinations. What nonsense. In practice, any field of experience meets our criteria. Remove the *and/*.

Because the *and/or* is usually just theoretical, most readers don't take the *and/or* seriously. They might stop taking the writer seriously, too. If you must seriously allow for multiple conditions, use the words *or both* at the end of the sentence:

We can meet our budget by increasing sales or cutting costs, *or both*.

8.7 Check Sentences for Misplaced or Dangling Modifiers.

To understand modifiers better, recall the basic English sentence, *Who does what*. A modifier is a word or a phrase that tells us something about the *who,* the *does,* or the *what.* Notice the modifiers in italics:

(who) The dog (does) buried (what) the shoe.
(who) The *yellow* dog (does) *quickly* buried (what) the *tattered old* shoe.

We need to follow two important rules to use modifiers. First, if we have a modifier in a sentence, we must have a *who* or a *does* or a *what* to modify. Second, we need to put the modifier next to the *who, does,* or *what*—not in the general neighborhood—but next to. Otherwise, we modify the wrong *who, does,* or *what.*

Misplaced modifiers often become the subject of jokes:

One morning I shot an elephant *in my pajamas.* How he got in my pajamas, I don't know. *–Animal Crackers* (1930).

Make sure that your modifier has a *who,* a *does,* or a *what* to modify. Otherwise you have a dangling modifier. Academic and scientific writers are prone to make this mistake because they want to avoid talking about themselves. In the sentence, *Having interviewed 100 veterinarians, cats are cleaner than dogs,* the phrase *Having interviewed 100 veterinarians* is a dangling modifier, unless the cats conducted the interviews.

The word *only* is a particularly troublesome and often misplaced modifier. For some reason, *only* always sounds better in the wrong place. Check every *only* in your text to ensure that you have *only* next to the word you want to modify. Consider the line in the famous love song by A. Dublin and H. Warren: "I *only* have eyes for you." The *only* can modify *I,* as in you are so ugly that I am the only person who can stand to look at you. Or, *only* can modify *have eyes,* as in you are pretty, but too stupid to listen to. If you want to change the sentence to be a compliment, you need to move the *only* next to the word *you:* I have eyes for *only* you, or I have eyes for you *only*.

Passive voice and ambiguous pronouns cause many of our modifier problems. If you fix the passive voice and the ambiguous pronouns, the modifier problems disappear. Here are three examples where passive voice or ambiguous pronouns are the culprit:

A recent White House report *was released* claiming that acid rain is a result of methane emissions by the President's scientific advisor. (How embarrassing for the advisor.)

Change to: The President's scientific advisor *released* a recent White House report claiming that acid rain is a result of methane emissions.

Two campers *were found* shot to death *by the park rangers*. (The park rangers I know are gentle people.)

Change to: The park rangers *found* two campers shot to death.

After measuring the rainfall, *there was* a flood watch. (Nothing in the sentence can measure the rainfall.)

Change to: After measuring the rainfall, the *weather service issued* a flood watch.

Despite *its* poor safety record, the city council awarded the contract to Acme Construction. (The city council is dangerous?)

Change the order: The city council awarded the contract to Acme Construction despite *its* poor safety record.

If you have a series of modifiers, you can't put them *all* next to the word modified. Sometimes, you can put the series in better order or separate the series with punctuation. In harder cases, you need to separate the modifiers into separate sentences:

John sat on the park bench *watching the squirrels drinking coffee and reading the newspaper.* (Sophisticated, caffeinated squirrels!)

Fix this problem with better order and punctuation: John sat on the park bench *drinking coffee, reading the newspaper, and watching the squirrels.*

I met a man *with a wooden leg named Smith.* What was the name of his other leg?—(From the 1964 Walt Disney film, *Mary Poppins*)

Order might help: I met a man *named Smith with a wooden leg.*

Or you can use two sentences: I met a man *named Smith.* He had a wooden leg.

The following are more examples of misplaced or dangling modifiers that amuse:

Our mixing bowl set is designed to please any cook *with a round bottom for efficient beating.* (Skinny cooks will not like this set.)

We want to hire a man to take care of our prize cow *that does not smoke or drink.* (Our cows that drink and smoke didn't win any prizes.)

The Fish and Game Club announced tuna are biting *off the west coast.* (California has some big, hungry tuna.)

After lying on the bottom of the Atlantic Ocean for 70 years, the photographers brought back pictures of the Titanic. (These photographers must love their work.)

Edit for Economy

Editing for economy—cutting useless words—takes time and effort. However, this edit saves time and effort for your reader, and you are more likely to get the result you want. French philosopher and mathematician Blaise Pascal wrote a famous postscript: "I would have written a shorter letter, but I did not have the time." True genius knows shorter is better.

When you edit for economy, cut useless words so the remaining, useful words have a greater impact. Your document becomes more clear, efficient, and vigorous. As an extra benefit, you reduce the number of grammar and punctuation errors. For example, when you cut a useless modifier, you don't need to worry if the modifier is in the wrong place. Use these seven techniques to find and cut useless words:

9.1 Cut useless verbs.
9.2 Cut useless prepositions.
9.3 Cut *who*, *which*, and *that*.
9.4 Cut useless repetition.
9.5 Cut redundancy.
9.6 Cut useless comments.
9.7 Cut useless modifiers.

After editing for clarity, you are ready to edit for economy. When you edited for clarity, you already cut many words—as many as 5 percent. Usually, you can cut another 10 to 40 percent of the words from your draft with no loss of meaning.

What causes so many useless words in our documents? We identify three causes: oral tradition, writing assignments, and manners.

Oral tradition. Speakers have always used extra words to slow the transmission of information. These extra words are useful in speech. The speaker can use the extra time to think of what to say next, and the listener can use the extra time to process the information just heard.

In written communication, extra words that slow the transmission are useless. The author has time to reflect and edit, and does not need extra words to create extra time that an extemporaneous speaker needs. Likewise, the reader can take time to reflect without the author adding extra words. Therefore, the extra words so often useful in speech are useless and distracting in the written form. The utility of extra words is a major distinction between spoken and written communication.

In the following examples, the spoken phrase is two to five times longer than necessary, creating a pause.

Sometimes useful when spoken	*Economical when written*
At this point in time	= now
Due to the fact that	= because
In the event of	= if, when
In order to determine	= to determine

Writing assignments. In school, our teachers gave us *minimum* length writing assignments. We learned the wrong lesson: long documents pass; short documents fail. Meanwhile, we were able to make our argument in half as many words as the teacher demanded. Therefore, we dutifully added extra words to make our mandatory word count. Most of those extra words were abstract, general, and useless. We got the false impression long sentences sound more sophisticated when in fact long sentences often indicate fuzzy thinking. After graduation when we write articles for publication, the editor gives us a *maximum* length.

By the way, if your professor, boss, client, or editor tells you to write a longer version of your document, write the same document to the *audience who knows little about the information—* see Step 1 ("Does the Audience Know Little or Much About the Information?"). Go through your document, paragraph by paragraph, and define your words. Provide examples, analogies, and pictures. Definitions, examples, analogies, and pictures add value and can more than double your word count. Extra words added just to increase word count are useless.

Manners. Good manners are useful, but do not overdo. When appropriate, use a few extra words in the introduction and conclusion of documents written for the sake of good manners. The classic *please* and *thank you* are necessary for good manners. However, too many words written for the sake of manners can backfire, sounding archaic, bureaucratic, or insincere: *We would like to take this opportunity to extend our most heartfelt and genuine gratitude. . . .* sounds insincere compared to a simple *Thank you.*

If you have trouble unraveling a wordy sentence, break the thought into simple *who does what* and *what does what* sentences. Ultimately, a word is useless if it does not help us understand *who does what* or *what does what*.

The rest of this section teaches seven techniques to find and cut useless words. Again, as the author, you are the best qualified to cut useless words. You know best whether the word is necessary.

9.1 Cut Useless Verbs.

When you edited for clarity, you already cut many useless verbs. The remaining useless verbs are usually abstract verbs; the concrete action comes from another verb buried inside a noun or a modifier. For example, *We must make a decision* becomes *We must decide.*

As students, we used buried verbs to increase word count. For example, take a simple sentence: *The partners agreed.* Only three words! So we bury the verb *agreed* in the noun *agreement* or the modifier *agreeable.* Now we can add more words, including useless verbs: *The partners found that they were in complete agreement,* or *The partners found that their decision was completely agreeable.* We more than tripled the word count, but we added zero value. Also, the longer sentence with buried verbs is dull and sounds bureaucratic.

To undo the damage of this bad habit, we need to find the actions buried in nouns and modifiers and use them as verbs. Often you find buried verbs by looking for these common suffixes:

Sample of suffixes	Example of buried verbs
–able	Advisable — advise
–ant	Compliant — comply
–ance	Performance — perform
–ation	Application — apply
–ence	Reference — refer
–ent	Dependent — depends
–ing	Maintaining — maintain
–ity	Prosperity — prosper
–ness	Forgiveness — forgive
–sion	Decision — decide
–tion	Suggestion — suggest

Compare the following text and note the improvement when we cut the useless verbs and instead use the verbs buried in the nouns:

We conducted an *investigation* of your business and made the *determination* that you are in *violation* of zoning laws. Specifically, you are involved in the *operation* of *breeding* dogs when your license limits *authorization* for the *operation* of a kennel. It is *necessary* that you bring your business into *compliance* by the *cessation* of your dog *breeding operation* or face *forfeiture* of your business license. (65 words)

Improved:

We *investigated* your business and *determine* that you *violate* zoning laws. Specifically, you *breed* dogs when your license is for a kennel only. You must *cease* dog breeding or *forfeit* your license. (32 words, or 50 percent fewer)

9.2 Cut Useless Prepositions.

English prepositions are numerous, troublesome, and often useless. We have much incentive and many opportunities to cut them.

Prepositions link a noun or pronoun to another part of the sentence. For example, *The rabbit ran out the gate.* The preposition *out* links *gate* to *ran.* Often, we can choose from many optional prepositions. For example, *minutes to, from, about, on, of . . . the meeting:* All are correct.

The large number of English prepositions is a problem. Depending on how you count, English has up to 150 prepositions. We don't need that many prepositions. Spanish has only 23 prepositions. Many English prepositions are synonyms. We can say the cat is *below, beneath, under, underneath* the table: four prepositions to tell us where to find the cat. Spanish needs one preposition for the job: *bajo.* Languages with fewer prepositions use them more precisely.

In contrast, English prepositions are chaotic, often causing genuine confusion. For example, my physics textbook has a chapter: "Newton's Second Law, The Acceleration *of* Gravity," but gravity does not accelerate. The author meant acceleration *due to* gravity or *caused by* gravity.

Many preposition controversies are petty. New Jersey folk stand *on* line to buy tickets. Virginians stand *in* line. Both are correct and both are idioms. Some prepositional uses are more standard. Typically we meet *at* an hour, *on* a day, *in* a month and year, *at* a building, *on* a street, *in* a city. Nevertheless, most people understand if we meet *in* a building *at* a street. Some editors get excited over the distinctions such as *compare with* and *compare to*. The rationale is that we compare similar things *with* each other and dissimilar things *to* each other. Okay, but the threshold for similar or dissimilar is often a matter of opinion.

Prepositions often provide the short pause in our oral communication. We write notes *down*. Then we go *back* to the office *in order* to type the notes *up*. If we type notes *up* all day *long*, we get tired *out*. Then we need to rest *up*. In this example, we cut the prepositions because they are stylistic flaws but not grammar errors: We write notes ~~down.~~ Then we go ~~back~~ to the office ~~in order~~ to type the notes ~~up~~.

You may end a sentence with a preposition; however, make sure the preposition is necessary and sounds natural. In the sentence, *Where are you from?*, the preposition *from* is necessary and sounds natural. The old Victorian phrasing, *From whence do you come?*, sounds unnatural.

The best defense against the confusion of English prepositions is to cut them. Then you don't need to worry whether the preposition is correct, and you avoid idioms. Instead of worrying whether you compare apples *with* or *to* oranges, cut the preposition—simply compare apples *and* oranges. Why worry which preposition to use in minutes *of the* meeting, *from the* meeting, *about the* meeting, *for the* meeting, *to the* meeting, or *on the* meeting . . . ? Cut the preposition to avoid the problem: the *meeting minutes*. If you need a preposition, try to use one word: Call ~~at~~ *about* 5 o'clock. Put the phone *on* ~~top of~~ the desk. Indicate ~~as to~~ *whether* ~~or not~~ . . . or better, Indicate *if*. . . .

Note how many extra words you can remove from the following text:

> Revenues *from* sale *of* lumber declined *by* 5 percent *in* the Third Quarter. Despite the fact *of* declining revenue, the sale *of* number *of* board feet rose *by* 15 percent. The decline *in* revenue was due *to* the fact that pressure *in* prices was caused *by* increased competition *from* suppliers *in* Canada. *In* the event *of* a further declines *in* the sale *of* lumber, the dividend *to* stockholders may be *at* risk *of* being cut. (75 words; 21 prepositions)

Improved text:

> Third quarter lumber revenues declined 5 percent, although board feet sales rose 15 percent. Canadian suppliers increased price competition. If revenue declines further, we may cut the stockholder dividend. (29 words, or 60 percent fewer; zero prepositions)

Don't sacrifice clarity when you cut prepositions. Consider the sign on the back of a moving truck: "Free Moving Videos!" Are the videos captive? Are they free-floating? Do they move you to tears? Or are they "Free Videos *About* Moving!" This sign needs the preposition *about*.

Cutting prepositions helps you avoid subject-verb agreement problems. For example, "Decide if any of these values need (*or needs*) to change," is problematic. Is the subject singular or plural? Cut the preposition: "Decide if any value needs to change." The subject *value* is obviously singular.

Make sure that if you still have a preposition in your sentence, the sentence is literally true. For example, you can literally *look up the chimney*. If the action is not literally true, pick another verb:

Look up my address.	(Look up my *what?*)	*Find* my address.
Take out insurance.	(Nobody is that lonely.)	B*uy* insurance.
Iron out our differences.	(That must hurt.)	*Settle* our differences.
Hold down a job.	(You hold it; I'll kick it.)	*Keep* a job.

By removing prepositions, you especially help readers who speak English as a second language.

9.3 Cut *Who*, *Which*, and *That*.

This edit cuts one of the frequent little pauses useful in speech but useless in documents. Cut *who, which*, and *that* when combined with a "to be" verb, because the words add no value to the sentence.

Usually, you simply strike the words:

Employees ~~who are~~ assigned to the new Jupiter Project must submit a form W-2 ~~that can be~~ found in the introduction packet ~~that was~~ issued during last month's orientation.

Sometimes you need to rearrange some words:
We must replace the copier *that is* obsolete.
We must replace the obsolete copier.

Sometimes the *which is* or *that is* accompanies other useless words. Don't be shy. Cut them all:

Remove the red safety tag, ~~which you will find~~ next to the oil drain plug.
Access the data ~~that will have already been~~ loaded onto your hard drive.

You can cut many other *which's* and *that's:*

Use the return envelope, ~~which~~ we provide.
Take all the time ~~that~~ you need.

However, do not sacrifice clarity. Sometimes we need the *that* to act as a barrier between two ideas that otherwise run together and confuse:

Economists warn [that] small businesses might suffer from new tax rules.

Are the economists warning small businesses about something? No. Therefore, we need the word *that* as a barrier to keep the ideas apart.

9.4 Cut Useless Repetition.

Before you cut repetition, decide if the repetition is useless. Often, repetition is a virtue, a coherence device to help the reader. But sometimes, the repetition is useless, even annoying. If so, you most likely have a series of like items.

Use two techniques to cut repetition from a series. First, you can combine sentences and thereby cut the repetition by at least half. Second, you can use a vertical list.

Combine sentences to cut repetition:

The *manufacture of vaccines* must use *FDA-approved* manufacturing and packaging *processes*. Furthermore, *the manufacture of vaccines* must store and ship vaccines following *FDA-approved processes*. (26 words)

Vaccine manufactures must use FDA–approved processes to manufacture, package, store, and ship vaccines. (14 words, or 46 percent fewer)

Use a vertical list to cut repetition:

To qualify for the $50 rebate, *you must* accomplish the following four steps. First, *you must* fill out completely and sign the accompanying 3-by-5 card. Second, *you must* attach the bar-code label as proof of purchase. Third, *you must* enclose the original cash register receipt—no photocopies allowed. And fourth, *you must* enclose a self-addressed stamped envelope. (57 words)

Revised:

To qualify for the $50 rebate, you must accomplish four steps:

1. Fill out completely and sign the accompanying 3-by-5 card.
2. Attach the bar-code label as proof of purchase.
3. Enclose the original cash register receipt—no photocopies allowed.
4. Enclose a self-addressed stamped envelope. (46 words, or 20 percent fewer)

Never use synonyms, passive voice, or ambiguous pronouns to avoid repetition. All three cause logical fallacies that in turn cause more damage to the document than repetition can cause.

9.5 Cut Redundancy.

Whereas repetition is often a virtue, redundancy is always bad, worse than useless. Redundancy means saying the same thing with different words, resulting in shifting words. Therefore, cut all redundancy.

If you begin a sentence *In other words,* you are already in trouble because you are about to use *other words* and confuse the reader. Rather than restate the same point with other words, add value by defining words and providing examples, analogies, and pictures.

Another cause of redundancy comes from doubling and tripling words, a bad habit that the English acquired after the eleventh century. For 400 years, much of English nobility spoke French. A few barons and the common folk spoke English. To accommodate both classes, lawyers wrote laws using key words from both languages: hence, *null and void. Null* is English; *void* is French. Other examples of legalese doubles include *aid and abet, full and complete, varied and sundry.* . . . For fun, ask a lawyer to explain the difference between *complete* disclosure and *full* disclosure.

Trying to sound like the educated lawyer class, the common folk doubled with phrases like *each and every, this day and age, appraise and determine, refuse and decline, clear and understandable.* People who double their words fall into a 500-year-old habit and sound like common folk posing as subject-matter experts.

Beware of word pairs joined by *and* or *or.* Cut the doubled words unless the reader needs both words.

> In this case, a refund is ~~right and~~ proper.
> Please ~~approve and~~ accept our offer.
> Doubling can ~~detract from and~~ confuse the message ~~or idea~~.
> We offer effective ~~and successful~~ methods.
> Attend this urgent ~~and important~~ meeting.
> We ~~acknowledge and~~ appreciate your contribution.

9.6 Cut Useless Comments.

Useless comments that you need to cut are often overly formal courtesies or statements of the obvious.

We cut useless words from these overly formal courtesies:

> ~~On behalf of the entire staff, I would like to take this opportunity to~~ thank you for your many years of ~~outstanding~~ service.
> ~~Perhaps it would be beneficial to take a moment and~~ read these instructions first.

Some wordy courtesies backfire, causing hard feelings:

As you may already know—If readers don't already know, you just
    called them *stupid*. A safer expression is, *This memo reminds* or
    Please remember.
All things considered—This cliché suggests something undisclosed
    is terribly wrong. You might as well write, *Despite his debilitat-*
    ing drinking problem. . . .
When you find time—These words imply that the reader can't
    manage time well. A safer expression is, *At your convenience.*

Don't restate the obvious. The reader already knows that most
things have a purpose, an intent, a goal, a design, or possibilities, so
most of those expressions are useless unless you are repeating for
emphasis.

~~The expressed purpose of~~ this report ~~is to, within the realm of~~
    ~~possibilities,~~ describe[s] ways to improve our employee health
    plan. (21 to 10 words)

The reader already knows that the document has an author.
Expressions like *It seems* and *It appears* tell us that the author is
aware. Of course the author is aware (or at least we hope the
author is aware). You can use qualifying phrases to highlight
your lack of conviction: *"In this special case, we suggest that. . . ."*
However, if too many sentences lack conviction, the document
loses credibility.

Avoid defining self-evident words such as *three feet ~~in length~~,*
red ~~in color,~~ ~~month of~~ June, and *~~subject of~~ chemistry* By cutting the
self-evident words, you get a 50 percent reduction in the follow-
ing sentence:

On ~~the form in question, called~~ FX-10, please write your claim
    number ~~in the blank space provided~~ on line 5. (20 to 10
    words)

9.7 Cut Useless Modifiers.

Modifiers are words we use to describe, limit, or otherwise alter the meaning of other words in a sentence. You already cut abstract and general modifiers when editing for clarity—words such as *very, great, extreme, several, dramatic, paramount, vital*.

Now, make another pass at your document to cut more useless modifiers. Most of these useless modifiers are clichés we hear every day. Speakers use these extra modifiers to slow the oral transmission. We need to cut them from our written prose.

> When we ~~finally~~ found the car, the battery was ~~obviously completely~~ dead. He ~~actually~~ left ~~both~~ the headlights on, which ~~totally~~ drained the battery ~~of all its power~~. (28 to 18 words)
>
> ~~At last,~~ the market survey was complete~~d in its entirety~~. The Market Committee reached a ~~full~~ consensus ~~of opinion~~. (19 to 11 words)

Many words describe an absolute; therefore, a modifier can add nothing. Here are a few more examples of useless modifiers of absolute words:

> *Absolutely* sure—not quite as sure as positively sure?
> *Almost* positive—usually means you are clueless
> *Complete* annihilation—much worse than partial annihilation
> *Honest* truth—as opposed to the dishonest truth
> *Most* unique—unique, uniquer, uniquest?

Cut useless modifiers that don't add information. Here are a few examples of useless modifiers already implied by the noun or verb:

Advance forward—to distinguish from advance backwards
Advance reservations—more useful than reservations for yesterday
Both cooperate—or you cooperate your way, I'll cooperate my way
Join *together*—more intimate than joining apart
Live performance—much livelier than the dead performance
Mutually agreeable—even disagreements are mutual
Previous experience—usually more credible than future experience
Unexpected surprise—more exciting than the expected surprise

Edit for Readability

Readability refers to how easy or difficult your document is to read. You can measure and control readability with three editing techniques:

10.1 Measure readability using the Gunning Fog Index.
10.2 Replace long words with short words.
10.3 Break long sentences.

You can measure readability with different algorithms: Flesch-Kincaid Grade Level, Flesch Reading Ease, and Robert Gunning Fog Index. Most word processors have a feature that automatically calculates readability. All readability algorithms measure the same two variables: word length and sentence length. Short sentences and short words are easier to read, so they improve the readability score. These algorithms typically present the score as a school grade level such as the twelfth grade.

Complex subjects do not cause complex language. In fact, if you have a complex subject, your readers need you to keep the language simple. If you have an audience who knows little about the information, you might need to write a longer document, but you also need to use shorter sentences and shorter words. All readers, whether they know little or much, want an easy-to-read document. They resent difficult words that send them to the dictionary. You cannot control the complexity of your subject, but you can control readability.

Making your document easy to read is not *dumbing down*. On the contrary, making complex subjects easy to read is the hallmark of successful communication. *Can Do Writing* has a readability score 8, meaning the language is suitable for a reader in the eighth grade—the preferred score of newspapers.

Writers who follow the *Can Do Writing* system achieve good readability. Sentence outlining ensures that the first sentences of your paragraphs are short. The edit for clarity shortens average sentence length. The edit to cut useless words also shortens sentences and words. For example, *Please send in your application* is four short words and one long word. *Please apply* has two short words and zero long words.

In this section, you learn how to check your document's readability with the Gunning Fog Index. If you need to lower your readability score, you can adjust the two variables: word length and sentence length.

10.1 Measure Readability Using the Gunning Fog Index.

The Gunning Fog Index is the easiest to calculate by hand. Work with a sample of a hundred words or more, always ending your sample at the end of a sentence. Don't include vertical lists in your sample. Lists cause a false reading for average sentence length.

Follow the formula in Figure 10.1.

Average sentence length	(105 words/5 sentences)	21
plus Long Words per 100	(12 words/100 count)	+12
		====
		33
multiply by constant 0.4		× 0.4
		====
equals Gunning Fog Index or grade level		13.2

Figure 10.1 Robert Gunning's algorithm for calculating readability

The Index value 13.2 is the grade level to which you wrote your document—college freshman in this case.

When counting long words per 100, count only words with three or more syllables. However, do not count proper nouns, acronyms, or Arabic numbers like 1998. Do not count *-es* or *-ed* endings as syllables. However, count *-ing* endings as syllables. For example, suceed*ed* counts as a two-syllable word, therefore, not a long word, but succeed*ing* counts as a three-syllable word, and therefore a long word.

Write at the level that your readers *want* to read, not at the level they *can* read.

Chart of readability levels is shown in Figure 10.2.

If you want to publish, make sure your readability matches your target publication. Editors have a keen sense of what their audience wants in terms of readability. If you write press releases, know your target publications, and stay at or below their readability. Also, people read 25 percent slower on the screen; therefore, when writing web-based documents, write at a readability lower by a grade or two.

| 6 | 7 | 8 | 9 | | 10 | 11 | 12 | | 13 | 14 | 15 | 16 |

- *USA Today*
- Shakespeare
  - *Hunt for Red October*
    - *Can Do Writing*
      - *Washington Post*
      - *New York Times*
                  - Trade Journals
                    - Peer Review Journals

Figure 10.2 Chart of readability levels

10.2 Replace Long Words with Short Words.

Limit your long words to 10 to 15 per 100 to keep your writing at a high-school level.

You and the reader are stuck with many long words that have no good short-word substitute, such as *civilization, helicopter, satellite,* and *computer.* Many professionals use long words that have a precise meaning in their work. For example, doctors writing for doctors use words like *inoculation for influenza* instead of *flu shot.*

Keep the long words that have no good short-word substitute. For example, don't replace the long word *sponsorship* with the short word *aegis.*

Replace other long words with one- or two-syllable words. Trust your natural speaking voice. Long words sound unnatural and overly formal. If you don't normally say the word to your intended audience, don't write the word.

If you can't avoid using long words, compensate by writing shorter sentences.

The following are two dozen examples of long words changed to one syllable words:

additional: more	operate: use
apparent: clear	optimum: best
demonstrate: show	preliminary: first
enumerate: count	probability: chance
expeditious: quick	represents: shows
expertise: skill	stratagem: plan
functionality: use	substantiate: prove
identical: same	terminate: end
magnitude: size	underutilize: waste
minimum: least	utilize: use
modification: change	variance: change
necessitate: need	verification: proof

Using short words is not dumbing down. Shakespeare used fewer than 5 percent long words.

10.3 Break Long Sentences.

If your readability score is too high because your sentences are too long, break sentences. Today, the average spoken sentence is 17 words. Professional writers keep average sentence length to less than 20 words, with most sentences in a range of 6 to 28 words. Even if your content is complex and words are necessarily technical, you can still control your sentence length.

Breaking long sentences is the fastest way to improve readability. If you cannot avoid a high number of long words, often the case in a scientific paper, you can always write shorter sentences and put your series into vertical lists.

You can break long sentences at punctuation. Punctuation often indicates a change in thought. You can use *who does what* and *what does what* patterns to untangle long, complicated sentences. In the next example, cut some useless words, and break sentences in the following text. Notice how improved readability and simple *who does what* pattern enlivens the text:

Although historians know that Blackbeard the pirate, also known as Edward Teach, was born in Bristol, England around 1680, they know little else about his earlier life except that he was capable of reading and writing, and literacy suggests that his family was of higher social standing, most likely middle class; he left Bristol for Jamaica to sail on the ships of privateers. (One sentence of 63 words, Grade 29)

Blackbeard the pirate was born Edward Teach in Bristol, England around 1680. His early life remains a mystery. He could read and write, which suggests he was middle class. He left Bristol for Jamaica to sail with privateers. (Average sentence length 10 words, Grade 7)

Make a separate sentence from parenthetical statements wedged inside the long sentence.

Your online bookkeeping account can generate reports (for example, cash flow, income statement, balance sheet, and depreciation schedules), pay bills, and sweep cash reserves into your money market account. (One sentence of 29 words, Grade 17)

Your online bookkeeping account can generate reports. Examples include cash flow, income statement, balance sheet, and depreciation schedules. Also, your account can pay bills and sweep cash reserves into your money market account. (Average sentence 11 words, Grade 9)

Again, using short sentences is not dumbing down. Leonardo da Vinci, in his notebooks, kept his average sentence to 17 words.

Conclusion

Congratulations!

You finished analyzing, writing, and editing your document for information and style. You still need to check for word choice, grammar, punctuation, and mechanics. Although *Can Do Writing* ends with editing, we leave you with a few helpful hints.

Because of your systematic editing, you have a head start on correctness. When writing your draft, you used *who does what* and *what does what* sentences. Therefore, your sentences are grammatically simple and less likely to have punctuation errors. Your edit for coherence already improved your document's consistency and mechanics. Your edits for clarity and economy solved many word choice and grammar errors.

You need a couple of resources to help you check for correctness. Buy a new dictionary every ten years. Words change—annoying perhaps, but true. Everyone in your office needs to work from the same dictionary.

Use a style manual appropriate to your work. Style manuals get into fine details, such as when to capitalize words. You have free access to the *Government Printing Office Style Guide* on the Internet. No style guide can answer every question. Therefore, if you create many documents, you need to supplement your chosen style guide with a *style sheet*. When you write for publication, ask for the publisher's style sheet, and use the publisher's chosen style manual.

Use your software tools, but don't trust them. Grammar checkers make mistakes. Autocorrect features cause embarrassments.

The Internet is a warehouse of information with on-line dictionaries, style guides, and tutorials on grammar and punctuation—plus search engines to help you find answers.

169

You know your subject matter. You have a proven system for writing. Now make good things happen for yourself and for your readers.

Have confidence in your documents. The *Can Do Writing* system works every time for every kind of nonfiction document. You can analyze any writing problem no matter how complex. You can organize your thoughts in the most persuasive manner to get the results you want because your readers get the results they want. One side benefit of using this system is that you become a better analyst—a clearer thinker!

Have confidence in yourself. By working systematically, you master the techniques. Each document becomes an opportunity to practice—to improve. Because you edit systematically, you quickly incorporate—hardwire, in effect—the techniques into your language. You naturally compose your drafts without passive voice, tense shifts, subjunctive mood, ambiguous pronouns, and other clarity problems. You naturally compose your draft using fewer useless words, and you naturally compose at a better level of readability. In just a few months, depending on how much you write, you notice that your drafts are cleaner.

Enjoy the efficiency of the system. You can better plan your time, and you can write 20 to 40 percent faster. Also, by using the purpose statement and outline, you can catch errors quickly and avoid painful rewrites.

Finally, take pride in the results of your work—not just the document, but your work. As a manager, take pride in your good decision made possible by your written policy. As a sales representative, take pride in your satisfied customers—the result of your proposal letters. As an engineer, take pride in your new technology, made possible by your design documents.

You *can do* it!

Index